Hermann Lotze, George Trumbull Ladd, Lewis Orsmond Brastow

Outlines of the philosophy of religion

dictated portions of the lectures of Hermann Lotze

Hermann Lotze, George Trumbull Ladd, Lewis Orsmond Brastow

Outlines of the philosophy of religion
dictated portions of the lectures of Hermann Lotze

ISBN/EAN: 9783743383548

Manufactured in Europe, USA, Canada, Australia, Japa

Cover: Foto ©Lupo / pixelio.de

Manufactured and distributed by brebook publishing software (www.brebook.com)

Hermann Lotze, George Trumbull Ladd, Lewis Orsmond Brastow

Outlines of the philosophy of religion

OUTLINES

OF THE

PHILOSOPHY OF RELIGION

DICTATED PORTIONS

OF THE

LECTURES OF HERMANN LOTZE

TRANSLATION EDITED BY

GEORGE T. LADD

PROFESSOR OF PHILOSOPHY IN YALE COLLEGE

BOSTON:
PUBLISHED BY GINN & COMPANY.
1895.

Entered, according to Act of Congress, in the year 1885, by
GEORGE T. LADD,
in the office of the Librarian of Congress, at Washington.

J. S. CUSHING & CO., PRINTERS, 115 HIGH STREET, BOSTON.

EDITOR'S PREFACE.

THIS translation of Lotze's 'Outlines of the Philosophy of Religion' is made from the German of the second edition, for the revision of which, as well as for that of the first German edition, Professor Rehnisch of Göttingen is responsible. In preference to the first edition, the second was selected, because it seems to be at once more compact (if that were possible) and more comprehensive. It is composed of the dictated portions of the Lectures given in the Summer-Semester of 1875 and the Winter-Semester of 1878–79. The first eight chapters belong to the earlier date; and, in fact, the course of 1875 closed with them. It was not until the year 1878 that Lotze added to this course the instruction on Religion and Morality (Chapter IX.) and on Dogmas and Confessions (Chapter X.).

In choosing this volume for the second place in the series of translations of these Outlines, I have been guided to a considerable extent by my own convenience as a teacher. It will be found to be very closely connected with, and indeed founded upon, the conclusions already made accessible in the translation of the 'Outlines of Metaphysic.' The Philosophy of Religion is, of course, primarily a speculative or theoretical treatment of the proofs for the Being of God, of his Attributes, and of his Relations to the World of matter and of finite spirits. But Lotze's metaphysical thinking leads him to the conclusion that the source and centre and sum of all that Reality with which it is the business of Metaphysic to deal, is the Personal Absolute whom — to use the language of Trendelenburg — "faith calls God." The Philosophy of Religion must therefore first derive from Metaphysic the results of a critical treatment of those assumptions concerning all that is Real, which enter into *all* experience; it must afterwards discuss these same assumptions in that expanded form which is the result of taking into the account the content of a *further* special experience of an æsthetic, ethical, and definitively religious kind. Readers who have not already made themselves somewhat familiar with the author's views on metaphysical questions, should, in studying this volume, recur constantly to the 'Outlines of Metaphysic,' or to the larger volume on Metaphysic in his 'System of Philosophy.'

It is my earnest hope that a large number of those whose work it is to teach religion will make a somewhat careful study of this brief philosophical treatise. It seems to me admirably adapted for an exercise in that fundamental thinking on the most important of subjects presented to the human reason, which no one can safely despise, and which few are in a position wisely to neglect. It is surely when applied to such subjects, if at all, that Philosophy may make good her claim to the ancient title which ascribed to her something of the 'divine.'

It is scarcely necessary for me to repeat what was said in the Preface to the 'Outlines of Metaphysic'; namely, that my office is solely that of an interpreter, and not at all that of a critic or judge, — favorable or unfavorable to any views of the author. One remark, however, may properly be added, simply with a view to guard those readers who are not familiar with the writings of Lotze, against impressions that might lead to misunderstanding him. This entire treatise is avowedly designed to inquire "how much of the content of religion may be discovered, proved, or at least confirmed, agreeably to reason" (see p. 2). It is an effort to treat of "Religion within the limits of mere reason." But it is also avowedly very far from that "barren rationalism" which overlooks the 'æsthetic' (in the widest sense) elements of human nature (p. 6 f.); it makes constant reference to, and attempts to afford satisfaction for, our indestructible religious needs. Particularly in the last two chapters, therefore, it should be remembered, that what may be said to be, 'speculatively' considered, either determinable or unknowable, is by no means necessarily the same when considered from the point of view occupied by the investigator of the specific truths of Biblical revelation. In other words, a large amount of speculative agnosticism is not incompatible with a firm conviction as to the truthfulness of the system of doctrines called Scriptural, and scientifically formulated by dogmatics.

The first translation of this volume, with the exception of Chapters II. to IV., was made by L. O. Brastow, D.D.: the editor is responsible for the translation of those three chapters and for the revision of the whole. The nature of both the subject and its treatment has made it possible to present this one of the series, with the exception of certain distinctively metaphysical portions, in a form more easily intelligible to most readers than was possible in the case of the 'Outlines of Metaphysic.'

GEORGE T. LADD.

NEW HAVEN, January, 1885.

TABLE OF CONTENTS.

	PAGE
INTRODUCTION	1
CHAPTER I. — The Proofs for the Existence of God .	8
II. — More precise Determinations of the Absolute	35
III. — The Metaphysical Attributes of God	45
IV. — Of the Personality of the Absolute .	55
V. — Of the Conception of Creation . . .	70
VI. — Of Preservation	81
VII. — Of Government	95
VIII. — Of the Conception of the World-Aim .	114
IX. — Religion and Morality . . .	129
X. — Dogmas and Confessions . . .	143

INTRODUCTION.

§ 1. If religion were a normal product of the human reason alone, then philosophy would be the sole legitimate organ for determining and interpreting its content.

If, on the contrary, it sprung from revelation, then reason alone would not be able, it is true, to have discovered it; but after it were in existence, it would still be necessary to show that its content is the adequate fulfilment for those religious needs which our reason is compelled to cherish, but would not be able of itself to satisfy. Even in this case, therefore, philosophy would have a work to accomplish by way of such authenticating. The assertion that the content of religion is a 'mystery' is not convincing. There can be many facts of religion of such sort that the possibility of their coming to pass may not admit of rational apprehension; and yet we should not without exception take offence at this. But a 'mystery,' the significance of which were not at least susceptible of definition, would be a mere curiosity devoid of all connection with our religious needs, and, on this account, an unworthy object of revelation.

Finally, if religion were a morbid product of the human spirit, philosophy, even in that case, would find occupation. It would have to investigate psychologically and historically the conditions of the origin of this delusion, as well as the conditions of avoiding it in the future.

The principal object of the following reflections is connected with the first point of view above suggested: that is, we seek to ascertain how much of the content of religion may be discovered, proved, or at least confirmed, agreeably to reason. The two other points of view we subordinate to this.

§ 2. It is customary to demand faith in contrast with knowledge as the proper organ for the truths of religion. Such an assertion finds its most exact expression in the intimation that, in fact, even scientific cognition always rests ultimately upon 'faith'; that is to say, upon an immediate act of trust in certain absolutely simple and self-evident truths, which are neither in need of any proof, nor capable of it.

An important distinction is overlooked in the above-mentioned view. All such ultimate, self-evident propositions, upon which our knowledge is founded, are general judgments, which do not tell us that anything whatever is or takes place, but which only declare what would exist or would have to take place, in case definite conditions occur; or — more concisely — they all merely express certain general rules, which we are obliged to follow in the combination of the content of our ideas. On the contrary, those propositions upon which the most special interest of religion depends, — for example, that God is, that He has created the world, that the soul survives death, etc., — are all of them declarative judgments, which assert a definite, particular fact. With respect to the before-mentioned general propositions, it may be understood that they are capable of being objects of our immediate insight or evidence; for they are nothing but expressions of the forms of activity, in which our reason according to its own nature must be exercised. On the other hand, these declarative propositions of faith, which assert a fact with respect to the ordering of the world that is foreign to our own nature, cannot with equal legitimacy be regarded as a natural or innate endowment of our spirit, but are in some sort the results of culture.

§ 3. It would be better to have undertaken a comparison of religious truth and scientific cognition different from the foregoing. No cognition consists merely of those general propositions of which we have made mention; but every cognition originates by means of the application of these propositions to a content which only experience can furnish; more concisely, it is an elaboration of given perceptions. Now it might be asserted that it is not the external world exclusively which furnishes these necessary data by influence on our senses. Rather is it quite as admissible to think of a divine or supersensible influence upon our interior being, by means of which 'intuitions' of another species fall to our lot, such as the senses can never supply, and such as constitute just that religious cognition which obtrudes itself upon us with immediate certainty.

It is to be said in reply to the foregoing claim that, although the aforesaid divine influences are willingly conceded, still, according to the analogy of the 'sense-impressions' which are brought into comparison with them, they can consist immediately in nothing but a certain mode of *our* affection, or of our experience, or of our feeling. Now, just as a sense-impression, — for example, a color or a tone, — is after all no 'cognition' whatever;

but such a cognition originates only by comparing one impression with others, and by noticing the relations which occur between them, just so would those supersensible impressions consist immediately in mere feelings, moods, or movements of our own mind; but they would still represent in this form no truth of religion. The rather would such a truth, as admits of being expressed in a definite communicable proposition, originate only through the agency of an elaboration in thought of those 'inner experiences' which go back to the 'grounds' of these states of the mind.

§ 4. The only remnant of any useful result from this opposition of science to faith is, therefore, the conviction that the whole of our knowledge certainly does not originate from external experience, which is mediated for us by the senses; but that there are also inner states which are available as data for the acquisition of truth. The finishing of the structure of religion depends, not exclusively but chiefly, upon these latter data; and of such inner states there may be distinguished three groups:—

(1) The personal feelings of fear, of absolute dependence on unknown powers, which belong to the most effective, but also to the most crude of the fundamental impulses that urge the mind to

seek consolation in a non-empirical view of the world.

(2) Then there are the much nobler and just as truly effective æsthetic feelings that yield themselves admiringly to the beautiful which they discover in the world, and by means of it are incited to form a picture of an ideal world. This they do without any egoistic interest in the consolation desired; but rather with the sure conviction that what is so fair and full of significance cannot be an accidental product of that which is without significance, but must be either the very Principle of the world or closely related to its creative principle.

(3) Finally, there are the ethical feelings, which, without being deducible from 'mere experience,' necessitate the attempt to think of the world as a system of affairs in which this fact of the moral obligation of the will to a definite form of action finds an intelligible and rational place.

If now we conceive of the truth of religion as developed from all these data by means of our reflection, then we certainly get at what might be designated as "Religion within the limits of mere reason," but still not at that which has been so called. For, in most attempts of this kind, the great and weighty influence of the aforesaid æsthetic elements is especially overlooked, and, thereby, a very barren rationalism takes the place of that which the whole reason, acting in all directions, would be able to produce.

CHAPTER I.

THE PROOFS FOR THE EXISTENCE OF GOD.

§ 5. The different attempts of reason to attain to certainty concerning the Supersensible, by starting from all the above-mentioned points of departure, are too manifold for direct statement. As often, however, as science has sought to give account of the results it has won, it has done this in a doctrine of the "Proofs for the existence of God." Accordingly we also now present these proofs with the design to show how each one of them adopts its own special method for discovering a portion of the supersensible truth; and with the brief preliminary remark that these proofs naturally cannot, properly speaking, demonstrate the existence of God as necessary, — that is, as dependent on something else, — but that they are all able merely to demonstrate our assumption of this existence as a logically necessary consequence of the given facts of the world.

§ 6. The ontological argument, as ordinarily apprehended, maintains that, while the conception of other beings does not include their existence, the conception of the most perfect Being of all does include it; and that this being would in fact contradict its own conception, if the one perfection — to wit, existence itself — did not belong to it.

The logical error of this argument is sufficiently well known. Not merely the conception of the most perfect Being, but indeed that of every living or active being (as, for example, the conception of an animal), includes existence also as necessary to be added in thought for defining it; and without this all the rest of its predicates (*e.g.*, sensation, motion, propagation, etc.) would be quite unthinkable. But with respect to no one of these conceptions, does it follow from the necessity of adding in thought this *mark* (of existence), that after this the total content of the conception thus fully thought has validity in the nature of reality also, and that it may not be a merely thinkable combination of our imagination.

But although logically this attempt at proof is quite invalid, it is nevertheless of interest in other respects. For that which induces it to regard existence as a necessary attribute of the total content of the conception of the most perfect Being, is not, as it is in the case of the other conception (that of the animal), the mere circumstance that the rest of the predicates would admit of formal attachment to what is existent only, and not to what is non-existent. This is obviously rather a case where an altogether immediate conviction breaks through into consciousness; to wit, the conviction that the totality of all that has value — all that is perfect, fair, and good — cannot possibly be homeless in the world or in the realm of actuality, but has the very best claim to be regarded by us as imperishable reality. This assurance, which properly has no need of proof, has sought to formulate itself, after a scholastic fashion, in the above-mentioned awkward argument.

§ 7. The cosmological argument begins in an apprehension of frequent occurrence, yet withal wholly incorrect; namely, that the existence of each individual Thing and of the world in general is contingent, and therefore presupposes not a contingent but a necessary Being. At this point, the particular conceptions which are wrongly attached to this thought, must be first subjected to a definition.

The ordinary use of language is not at all acquainted with the philosophic significance of the word 'contingent,' according to which it is applicable to every existing thing whose non-existence in general would be thinkable without contradiction, and whose conception or whose nature accordingly offers no resistance to the cessation of its own existence. Rather does the common usage in the first instance merely contrast the 'contingent' with the designed, and understands by it all those secondary effects which, without being themselves designed, originate from action of ours that is designed. This happens because our actions themselves are for the most part capable of accomplishment only by means of some change in the objects of the external world; these objects, however, because of those relations independent of ourselves in which they stand to each other, cannot be changed by us without propagating still further in various directions the impressions they have received.

We speak, furthermore, of 'contingent' events, when we have directed our attention to a general law of nature and when, in its application to a single case, processes occur which do not follow from the law and from the circumstances necessary for its application, but only from the accessory circumstances that are foreign to the law. Even such a 'contingent,' as well as the preceding, is, wherever it occurs, necessary and inevitable, and is constantly conditioned by its own adequate reasons; only these reasons do not reside in the design nor in the law.

Finally, we also call such facts 'contingent' as

are assumed by us not to be predestinated in such a plan of the world's course as we have rightly or wrongly presupposed, but only to originate incidentally through the mechanism of those efficient agencies which are summoned for the accomplishment of that plan.

And with the one just mentioned is connected the still broader use of the word, according to which it becomes a mere determination of value, and designates that whose nature and content seem to deserve existence neither on account of its own value nor by connection with other values; although it, nevertheless, is in possession of such existence. In this sense, the 'contingent' is simply the matter of fact, whose being does not permit either of derivation from an effectuating condition, or of justification by its own value.

§ 8. The other conception, namely, that of the 'necessary,' is, in the only meaning of it which is quite clear to us, completely identical with that of the 'conditioned.' That only 'is' *necessary*, the actuality of which cannot be conceived of as lacking, whenever a definite presupposed condition actually takes place.

But it is very easy to understand whence comes the wish to place in opposition to this "conditioned necessary" another of a higher sort. For a given c, which must of course exist in case a determinate b exists, is 'necessary' only in the sense of its being *forced*. By means of its own nature merely, and without the aid of b, this c would *not* exist. The 'necessary' in that higher sense which is sought, would therefore be such an one as is not dependent on anything else for its existence, and consequently is not conditioned.

But it is entirely incorrect to persist in designating such an unconditioned as is sought for, by the predicate 'necessary.' It must rather be called the absolute matter of fact, which exists for the reason merely that it does exist; which does not need for its existence any extraneous condition; but which, for precisely this reason, can only be an actual and never a necessary existence.

§ 9. According to the analysis made above, the thoughts of the cosmological argument do not cohere well. From the so-called 'contingent,' — *i.e.* from that which is conditioned by something else external to it, and in just this respect must be called likewise *necessary*, — it is certainly possible to ascend to the Unconditioned, whose existence is dependent on nothing else; but for this very reason such an unconditioned is not 'necessary,' but merely matter of fact or actual. The desire to find something, which by means of its own nature, made its own existence necessary, is intrinsically beyond the possibility of realization, — as we saw it to be in the case of the ontological argument; and to this cause was due also the failure of the thought that the Unconditioned which is sought is to be found in a most perfect Being. To that merely actual (not necessary) unconditioned existence, the smallest, meanest, and most insignificant thing has just as good a claim as the most perfect; and that precisely for the reason that it is an unconditioned existence, and therefore is dependent on no reasons of any kind.

In another direction also the cosmological argument goes farther than its premises permit. It was legitimate to seek an Unconditioned for the Conditioned in the world; but it is an altogether arbitrary leap to assume that this Unconditioned must be *One;* and, furthermore, that it can be conceived of only in the form of a single real Being. It is possible that this assumption may be justified subsequently; but just at this point the other assumption, to which the natural sciences have come through their need of interpreting the world, obviously lies much nearer at hand. We refer to the assumption of a very great multiplicity of unconditionally existing elements, which are independent of each other, and are only subject to a general sphere of laws in accordance with which the manifold phenomena proceed from their changeable positions with respect to each other.

One more consideration of a logical character must first qualify this view. It is that we get no insight as to how a single unconditioned being, even though it were in existence, would be able to condition anything else, and therefore serve as the desired initial member in the conditioned series of the world's events. A conclusion or a consequence never follows except from the concurrence of two premises, and not from one premise alone. To the one unconditioned Being, therefore, if aught is to result from it, there would always have to be added again other accessory circumstances, which do not emanate from it, but which are just as much unconditioned: the world therefore would not be dependent upon *one*, but upon *many* unconditioned beginnings.

§ 10. The teleological argument proposes to make that empirical conformity to an end, which appears in the world, the point of departure for an inference with respect to a single designing and creative reason, as the supreme cause of the world.

Let us in the first place investigate the conception of that which is 'conformable to an end,' as such. This conception is entirely free from ambiguity only when we take our start from the conscious purposes of our own will, which are fixed upon a determinate result as their end. In that case, what is 'conformable to an end' is the selection or combination of means, which, by their legitimate action, bring about the realization of the aforesaid end. To call those means themselves 'conformable to an end' is, properly speaking, not correct. They are themselves merely serviceable: that is to say, their nature is *in itself* calculated for no determinate end whatever, such as we might set for ourselves; but it is merely of such sort that a useful application of it to our ends becomes possible for us.

Now that this 'serviceableness' or 'accidental conformity' of things in the world to an end, is of very frequent occurrence, proves nothing further. For when once there exist Things with properties of their own and with established methods of action, it is a matter of course that some of our designs (which themselves, in the last analysis, always amount to the same as some alteration in the states of Things) may be accomplished by means of the activity to which other Things lay claim. More than this, however, does not in reality take place. The nature of Things is not so eminently useful, that it would be sufficient for the accomplishment even of all authorized designs; and it is not so absolutely useful that it might not serve just as well for the frustration of that which is rational, and for the production of that which is unauthorized.

§ 11. In contrast with the aforesaid utility, an "immanent conformity to an end" is spoken of, which appears primarily in the individual organisms that have no other end beyond their own existence, but in each one of which all parts are reciprocally related as end and means. Such conformity to an end is then transferred from these individual organisms to the Universe, as to a "great organism."

Now we are accustomed to assert that these composite forms cannot possibly be mere products of the blind co-operation of many elements, without the unity of one controlling design. Such a conclusion is decidedly false. Even supposing a conscious design to be demonstrably at work, still the realization of its end is always dependent on the fact, that every particle of this end is likewise the inevitable and undesignedly necessary product of the co-operation of the means summoned to aid. The end would not be possible at all if it were impossible in accordance with the laws of the mechanism which these means follow; and it would not be actual, if it were not also necessary in accordance with these laws, at the very instant when the aforesaid means are applied.

But still further: It is supposed that at least the bringing together of the means themselves, into those positions in which they are of necessity compelled to realize the end, is impossible without a controlling design. But again it may be answered: Even where this design actually exists, it is unable to bring the usable means into those useful positions by its own mere volition; on the contrary, it is able to accomplish this only by summoning physical agencies and forces of a sort similar to the means themselves. Therefore the state attained at any given instant, when the end is accomplished, must be regarded as the necessary resultant of the co-operation of these forces at the preceding instant; and instead of an intelligence which might explain the state of the case belonging to this preceding instant, there may always be substituted a combination of other blind elements and forces which were compelled to have precisely the same result.

To state the same thing briefly: The completely automatic blind origin even of the system most conformable to an end, is never impossible; it is only improbable. And now the question comes, what is meant by this latter expression?

§ 12. If we take for granted, that an indefinite multitude of different elements act upon one another entirely in accordance with mechanical laws, and that they were aboriginally in reciprocal motions which were not regulated by any design, then there might issue from such conditions innumerable possible consequences. The forms possessed of an immanent conformity to an end would represent only a very insignificant number among these possible consequences; and therefore they would have very little probability of coming into existence. But to reason back from this to a design proposing an end, would be valid only in case the forms conformable to the end alone appeared in the world; and in case those other results that are without an end, or in contradiction to an end, were neither present in experience, nor needed to be assumed even as having existed in the past.

Neither of the above-mentioned suppositions corresponds with the facts. In our actual observation there occur innumerable cases of disease and of the failure of rational life-ends;—to say nothing whatever of the very many facts and occurrences which, so far as our discernment extends, are at least without an end, even if they disturb no other end. But with reference to the past we are at liberty to assume, that at first an innumerable multitude of inharmonious forms, intrinsically hostile to any end, actually emerged from the reciprocal impact of blind elements; that these forms, however, were not able to maintain themselves in the course of nature, as against the constant assaults from without; that, on the contrary, only those few held out, which had chanced to be the more fortunate; that then these fortunate ones exerted more and more a determining influence upon the rest; and that thus gradually it has come to pass, that nature runs its course, not indeed in complete perfection and conformity to an end, but after all to such an extent that there still remain but few disturbances or interferences by which the development and perpetuation of the structures that are conformable to an end, is endangered. In this way, therefore, it would not be unthinkable that an original chaos gradually shaped itself into a nature that is arranged in conformity to ends.

§ 13. Moreover, it is not necessary to stop with the altogether meagre assumptions which we have made. If it is once held to be conceivable that a single supreme intelligence may exert an influence upon the reciprocal relations of the elements of the world, then similar intelligence may also be imagined as immediately active in all these individual elements themselves; and, instead of conceiving them as controlled merely by blindly operative forces, they may be imagined as animated spiritual beings, who strive after certain states and offer resistance to certain other states. In such case there may be imagined the gradual origin of ever more perfect relations, from the reciprocal action of these elements, almost like the reciprocal action of a human society; and that too without necessarily arriving at the assumption, to which we are here inclined, of a single, supreme, intelligent Being. Our reasoning issues rather in a sort of polytheistic or even pantheistic conception, and that too in quite tolerable agreement with experience.

§ 14. Against what was said above it may still be objected, that the persistence, the power of self-maintenance, and the equipoise of the more fortunate forms, which we previously admitted to have originated in the blind course of nature, are not identical with that conformity to an end, the admiration for which was our point of departure in the teleological argument. The aforesaid mere equipoise, and the permanence that originates from it, might also belong of themselves to altogether purposeless forms; that is to say, to forms whose entire existence would have absolutely no immediate value and no rational significance. Both these characteristics however we suppose we recognize in those structures conformable to an end, which we are here making our point of departure.

There is a remainder of truth in the above-mentioned view; but the thought does not prove what it was assumed to prove. To wit, so soon as we confine ourselves simply to admiration for an immanent conformity to an end, we are in fact scarcely ever able to demonstrate conclusively that the total result which is produced by it is actually anything of absolute value; — a value which would have to be apprehended either as being generically its own end, or as being such an end as to admit of our understanding that it could have been devised only by a designing wisdom, and that it only, rather than one of its opposites, was worthy of this wisdom.

We admire, for example, the stability of the planetary system; we believe that only a Providence has been able to choose from among the innumerable possible arrangements of its masses, precisely that one on which this stability depends. But it may be questioned whether after all this constant repetition of the same occurrences is, as a matter of course, a supreme end; and whether it may not rather be a tedious arrangement; so much so that there might conceivably have been innumerable arrangements, that never occur in the actual world, which the one succession of different developments of the heavenly bodies might have established, — something much more manifold, novel, and interesting. In plants, after they once exist, everything harmonizes as means and end. But what is the value of their entire existence? Ends external to themselves, which they serve, are accomplished by them; but they might possibly have been accomplished by a shorter method. Their own growth and bloom is in the estimate of our understanding an entirely purposeless fact, in which nothing further actually appears than that equipoise which the mechanical course of nature is capable of producing, and from which the conformity to an end here assumed should be quite essentially distinguished.

The above-mentioned consideration may be extended to the world of animals and men: so long as there are still among the latter so many complaints about unrealizable ideals, the thought that much of the beauty we conceive has no existence will continue to nullify the conclusiveness of the teleological argument.

§ 15. If we summarize our thoughts, there remains but one point of a positive character, and this is the conviction that there is in the world at all events a great deal of that which is beautiful and great and excellent, — admiration for which was the point of departure for this teleological argument; and that it is by no means possible to get rid of this argument by deducing all its examples from the undesigned reciprocal actions of innumerable elements, working in accordance with law. By such deduction we merely change the location of that which has value. We are necessitated then to assert of just that aforesaid original nature of the elements, and of their general laws of action, that they themselves from the very first include within themselves the ground capable of developing that which has value.

But the course of thought given above has utterly failed as an argument for the existence of God. That Intelligence, of which we cannot be wholly rid, admits just as well of being apprehended as a property adhering immanently to all Things; or even, if one is pleased to seek it outside of Things, as a multiplicity of spiritual beings or demons, who share with each other in the creation and control of the world. And each of these assumptions really harmonizes better with the immediate impression of experience than the hasty assumption of one only supreme wisdom, from which as their source the imperfections of the world, that in fact are manifest to us, are much more difficult to comprehend.

§ 16. The teleological argument was wrecked by the fact that it was unable, with sufficient certainty and to a sufficient extent, to prove empirically the empirical datum, which it assumed to make its point of departure, — namely, the world's conformity to an end.

We attempt therefore to find our point of departure in a simpler datum, which is not so doubtful, and which is quite as generally acknowledged. And we attempt to deduce from it, not exactly the existence of God, but a more modest conclusion, which shall serve us as a preliminary condition for that other conclusion.

This datum is in substance the assumption that all the elements of the world, without exception, act upon each other, no matter whether adapted to an end or the reverse; and therefore that each exerts influences upon the rest, or, in turn, receives influences from them. So far as our experience extends, it confirms this assumption. The objection against it, that we know little of the past, and absolutely nothing of the future, and that even in the present perhaps individual elements do not stand in any relation of reciprocal action with each other, cannot refute the assumption. For this indifference just mentioned between two elements — a and b — at the same time that each individual element stands in a relation of reciprocal action with many others, we should after all never be compelled to regard as a fact based upon no principle, but as the necessary consequence of the same 'law,' in accordance with which a and b exercise the aforesaid other reciprocal actions. And just so, if in the past or future these actions of the elements with respect to each other, were different from what they are now; yet we should not regard even this as a fact independent of conditions, but as conditioned by some fixed law, which sooner or later would demand other actions with the same consistency with which it now demands the ones in question.

If what was said above be not acknowledged, but if it were maintained rather that the elements of the world, without any cause, have sometimes acted upon each other, in general, and at other times not at all, at one time thus and at another time otherwise; then the very basis for every investigation would be abolished. Such a world would furnish no data whatever for any conclusion, even with respect to an event that is to be anticipated within its own limits merely, still less for any conclusion with respect to anything external to itself, which might be regarded, as in any sense, its ground, its cause, its end, or its principle.

§ 17. From the foregoing it follows now that the individual elements, of which the world is composed, are by no means able to exist as they will; and that therefore a course of the world cannot be deduced from real beings, which are from the beginning wholly without relation to each other.

If, for example, all things were as incomparable with each other or as disparate as perhaps 'red' or 'sweet' (and nothing would prevent the making of such an assumption, in case each real being is completely independent, and has to pay no regard whatever to all the others), it is evident that no definite result could possibly spring from any relation between two such beings (supposing one to be at all able to conceive of such a 'relation') with any more right than any other could claim. For, in order that the result m must originate from a and b, while the same result m could not originate from a and c, it is necessary that there first exist between b and c, not a complete incomparability, but a definite contrariety, or a difference of definite magnitude, — a thing which is not thinkable, unless b and c are comparable.

The further development of these considerations would show then, that this comparability must obtain, not merely between b and c, but between *all* the real elements of the world; and this in such manner, that these elements constitute collectively, not members of a single series, indeed, but rather members of a system of series intersecting each other; and also in such manner that it should be possible for one to proceed from the nature of each individual element to the nature of every other, by a definite number of steps, taken within this network of system. Such a state of the case lies, as a silent assumption, just as if it were utterly impossible to be otherwise, at the foundation of our entire view of the world; and, on this account, the importance of this wonderful circumstance is commonly overlooked.

§ 18. It would be over-rash to infer from this, without further question, a common origin for all these elements. For although this comparableness of theirs seems like a single select case from among many in contrast with the empty possibilities which we might be able to imagine (as, for example, that all the elements were as totally different as 'red,' 'sweet,' or 'warm'), nevertheless there is applicable to the case no calculation of probabilities, in accordance with which it would be impossible to accept the existence of this particular case as a mere matter of fact independently of a common cause for all the elements.

On the contrary, a different conclusion is justified. It is not enough that the natures of Things are homogeneous, unless the same natures stand in some other connection besides. From such homogeneity it would barely follow what result (c) must originate from the meeting of two beings a and b,—taking it for granted that there were in general some reason why something new must originate, and why the mere existence of a and b and their conjunction could not have been enough. Or, as expressed in other words: The most that follows from the comparable natures a and b concerns the result which they are necessitated to produce, or the manner in which they are necessitated to act upon one another; but it does not follow that they must produce anything whatever, or that they must act at all upon each other.

In case we draw a conclusion c from two premises a and b, the meaning is as follows: In the unity of our thinking *ego*, the two thoughts a and b cannot appear as states of this ego without the thought c being attached to them, — and this just on account of the nature of this one subject. If, on the other hand, the thought a were conceived by one person, and the thought b by another, then the thought c would not originate as a consequence in either one of the two, although c, and c alone, would be the necessary result of a and b *provided* they came together at all. The case is exactly so with *Things*. From the mere fact that one Thing a exists, and another b exists, c does not by any means follow, of course; and this, although c would be the only effect which could follow, provided a and b acted upon each other. We must investigate the question what, in such a case, would correspond to that identity of the thinking subject by means of which the thoughts a and b alone are necessitated to produce a result.

§ 19. We derive from Metaphysic the conviction, that this fact of the reciprocal influence of two Things a and b is impossible, so long as both were conceived of as entirely self-sufficient and in such sort independent of each other, that a might exist and be what it is, even though b had no existence. It remains a completely insolvable contradiction, that a and b accommodate themselves to each other (that b, therefore, enters into a state β, as soon as a enters into the state α), if a and b have no concern with each other.

We derive moreover from Metaphysic the further conviction, that all middle terms, which are interpolated between a and b, such as the 'transition' of a 'substance,' of an 'influence,' or of a 'force,' are either essentially inconceivable ideas, or at any rate do not at all explain the action, but always leave unanswered the same question; namely, how x after its transition from a to b can begin the production of a change in b, — that is to say, how x can act upon b, or how in general one Thing can act upon another.

Finally, we derive the conviction that the aforesaid inconceivableness can be removed only by the negation of the independence of individual Things: a and b cannot be absolutely different beings, but only modifications of one and the same Being M, which is in them all, in a, b, c, d, . . ., the truly Existent; and which has indeed assumed different forms in all these different Things, but still remains indivisibly one and the same individual M.

If, then, in the single Thing a there occurs a

change a, this a is *co ipso*, is of itself already besides a change of M, and has no need first to become such a change. If then we conceive the nature of M as always endeavoring to maintain its own identity, M will now produce within itself a second state β, which occurs as a compensation to a, and in connection with it forms again an expression of the whole nature of M.

It is not necessary, however, that this β should appear in our observation as a change of a, but it may appear as a change of the other individual Thing b. And this would then be the procedure which we conceive as an "action of a upon b."

§ 20. For the sake of elucidation the following remark must be added: What this one Being, or — according to the common expression — what 'the Absolute' is, remains at first completely indeterminate. From the fact of the reciprocal action of individual Things, the only conclusion at which we arrived was that of the necessary unity of this Absolute. What it is, is left for further determination.

Furthermore, in designating Things as "modifications of the Absolute," it is to be acknowledged that such an expression contains no explanation whatever of the precise sort of unity which obtains between Things and the Absolute; or of the sort of dependence in which they stand with reference to that Absolute. The expression has rather the distinct negative meaning which denies the self-dependence of individual Things. With something of like sort we are frequently compelled to be satisfied. We are very often obliged, for the purpose of removing a contradiction or of explaining an occurrence, to postulate a fact, with respect to which, however, we are never able to say how it were possible for it to exist, or to have been brought to pass; — and this, even in case it can be yet more accurately defined than the fact that is just now assumed by us. We postpone to a subsequent chapter whatever more there is to be said upon this point.

Finally; even the elasticity, or self-maintenance, that we attribute to the Absolute, is used in a preliminary way merely as a not unimaginable expression to which different significations may be given. It is not necessary to conceive of the reactions of the Absolute against the changes that occur, as directed, in a merely mechanical way, to the preservation of the *status quo;* instead of this, we might assume even an impulse of development in progress towards a definite goal; and that this impulse, likewise, by means of any state α which had originated either elsewhere or in the prosecution of this purposeful activity, would occasion the production of a further state β, by which such purposeful activity would be propagated further. Such an assumption, made in a preliminary way, is a matter of indifference. It is certain only that if there is to be any reciprocal action whatever of individual Things, there must be in the Absolute some such consistent sensibility as is necessitated to produce by means of α its consequence β, no matter whether it be for self-maintenance or for progress.

CHAPTER II.

MORE PRECISE DETERMINATIONS OF THE ABSOLUTE.

§ 21. It is not our present design to dissect logically the conception of an 'Absolute,' and to lay down the conditions under which aught would be held to be the Absolute or acknowledged as such. As far as this is a matter of interest, it is too difficult for the present moment. Just now we are rather making the attempt to specify by name that which is by its own nature adapted to fulfil the conditions above alluded to; and, of course, fulfil them in such a way that it can be recognized as the absolute Principle of that world which is given in experience as bare matter of fact. Not to stray too far abroad, we confine ourselves to the two contraries between which it has long been customary to distribute the consistence of whatever is actual; namely, Matter and Spirit.

§ 22. The assumption that the common substance of the world is only *matter*, and matter as endowed only with those properties which we in physical science attribute to every portion of the same, has probably never been made in earnest by any one.

Such an assumption would take upon itself the difficult problem of showing how, from these mere properties of space-filling, inertia, divisibility, and mobility, all the rest of the world, and therefore even its spiritual constituents, could be developed as a matter of course, — that is to say, as the mere consequences of such properties and without admixture of any other principle whatever.

Now Psychology has compelled us to the conviction that the states of motion — which can only be considered as events that happen to masses of the kind referred to above — are, as a matter of fact, the occasions upon which there arise *in us* spiritual processes, such as sensations or feelings. But in what way these occasions bring after them these results so unlike themselves, is not only not a subject of empirical knowledge, but it is even possible to see that we can never reach the point where it would be for us a matter of course that a mode of the motion of these masses, however wondrously intricate, would now have to cease to remain such, and would be necessitated to transmute itself into quite a different process, of sensation or of feeling. According to all the axioms of which we avail ourselves elsewhere in the mechanical consideration of nature, from *motions* alone nothing but a transference, new distribution, propagation or arrest, of *motions* can originate. A spiritual effect can be attached to them only indirectly; to wit, by means of the action of the aforesaid physical processes on a subject which, in its own nature, possesses that capacity for the production of psychical processes in which the motions themselves are wanting.

As here in the small, so also in the totality of the world, a Principle of barely material nature would be in no condition to produce from itself the world of spiritual processes.

§ 23. Now although each of these two series of events, the spiritual and the physical processes, requires its own peculiar 'ground' in reality, it is nevertheless not necessary that the 'ground' of the two be divided into two different species of reality, in such a manner that there may be material Things devoid of all spiritual susceptibility, and spirits devoid of all physical property and activity. The rather may we first examine the thought that both of these original properties are in fact inseparably united in every existence; and that, on account of one of them, the Existent is able to appear as, and to pass for, matter; while, on account of the other, contrariwise, it leads an inner life and develops spiritual states within itself.

For the psychology of the individual being, this assumption, on closer inspection, is shown to be unproductive. For the consideration of the world as a whole it, at first, has more to recommend it; and it forms the text of the spirited descriptions in which Pantheism glorifies the unresting life of the eternally One Substance, both corporal and spiritual, which in ceaseless vicissitude fashions its individual shapes, and lets them be absorbed again into itself.

The more definite formulating of these thoughts, in the case of Spinoza and Schelling, arouses our scruples against them. When the former (Spinoza) ascribes to the Absolute innumerable kinds of doing and acting ('Attributes') that admit of no comparison with each other, — of which, to be sure, only two, namely Thought and Extension (*cogitatio* and *extensio*) are familiar to us men, — such manifoldness obviates in some degree, at least for the imagination, the difficulty which lies in the singular circumstance, that just those two attributes which are not reducible to each other are assumed to form the essence of all the Existent. To find, however, for both of these attributes a still 'higher common root,' from which both issued as mere consequences, but did not themselves constitute such root (so Schelling,) is a problem that surpasses all human power of comprehension. It is indeed possible to fashion the name of such a 'First Absolute,' which is neither real nor ideal, and yet is the ground of both. But it is not possible to discover anything in the entire world, of which it could be said that it belongs to *this* thing, by virtue of its own nature, to be esteemed as such a common root.

Since, therefore, the goad of this Dualism cannot be got rid of, and a substance that is merely real and acts blindly does not suffice for explaining the world, we find herein one of the motives that lead us to the opposite attempt, — to the pure Spiritualism which undertakes to comprehend the spirit alone as truly existent, and all else as its product.

§ 24. The above-mentioned views, on being carried out further, are wont by preference to invalidate yet more the spiritual element of the Absolute. Such views customarily announce this element as a reason that is '*per se* unconscious'; that only in individual points of its extreme altitude, in individual spiritual beings, raises itself to consciousness.

Such a form of conception as the foregoing appears inadmissible. We have no right to strip off from the Reason, which we invariably first learn by experience to know as conscious, this predicate of consciousness, and then persuade ourselves that aught intelligible is left still remaining. Rather is it true that only one definite thought admits of being connected with the expression, a reason acting unconsciously in the world; to wit, the thought that *blind* forces act in the world, which are not in any respect reason, but which in fact act so that their results are the same as those which a reason acting in the world would have been compelled to desire.

At this point the additional misfortune comes to view, that the aforesaid proposition does not admit of being proved with reference to any kind of nature's action. For, in order to do this, it were necessary to show that the results of her action are the fulfilment of those absolute ends which reason would have been, not merely *able* to propose to itself, but *compelled* to propose as the ones justified in the highest degree. If, on the contrary, we appraise what is actually achieved in nature at a lower value, and assume that it *could* have been still better, but is not so, then we should be quite as much justified in speaking of an *un*reason acting blindly in the world.

But apart from this, it is clear according to what was said above, that a self-conscious reason could never originate as a final product from such powers; rather should we have to be satisfied with unconsciousness throughout the entire world.

It is wrong also to appeal to the analogy of our own spirit, which, without conscious design, instinctively produces many of its rational works; such, for example, as those of art. We admit the existence of such activities; but we know of them in absolutely no other case than that of spirits whose nature it is to be self-conscious: moreover, they appear in this case as actions accompanying or following excitations and states which were originally possible only in consciousness, but which in time vanish from consciousness by reciprocal inhibition. How, on the other hand, anything similar could take place in a subject, in whose nature no consciousness had ever preceded such activities, is not in the slightest degree comprehensible.

§ 25. In connection herewith, the same view is fond of speaking of an *impersonal* Spirit.

This, too, is much easier to say than by it mentally to represent anything. It is quite correct that, in our own spiritual life, we experience manifold states in which all attention to our own self, and all positing of that self over opposite to an external world, are completely gone; and we so lose ourselves in the content of a sensation, an idea, a feeling, or an effort, that we (so to speak) *are* for a time nothing but this, as it were, self-apprehending content, and not a subject which had this content as an object of its consciousness and distinguished it from itself.

But it is just as certain that we know such states only as occurrences in an otherwise personal spirit. They merely prove that it is not necessary for the personal spirit at every moment to think of itself as different from the content which exactly fills out its consciousness. But they cannot prove that anything similar is possible without the personality, which, in such a case, does not indeed mentally represent itself, but none the less remains in fact the condition of the possibility of such a self-forgetfulness. For all the aforesaid sensations, ideas, or feelings, in which we thus lose ourselves, are after all never thinkable except as states of a definite, self-identical and separate spiritual subject; and not the least consecutiveness, nor any coherency according to law between these different spiritual states, would be possible, unless the personal unity of the spirit, which is by no means apparent in them, were for all that the real ground which unites them with one another.

§ 26. It is further adduced in support of the above-mentioned view that even *the* 'personality' with which we have an acquaintance, — to wit, that of the human soul, — first originates in the course of its development. As originally given there exist, it is said, only common spiritual capacities which, by means of favorable circumstances, are aroused to expression in such manner that, from the combination of these expressions, a reflection directed toward self and a self-consciousness can also originate.

Just so, it is claimed, the Absolute at first is *impersonal* Spirit. At this point views are divided: one makes the Absolute, just like the finite spirit, attain to a personality of its own; the other makes it always remain of itself impersonal and only assume personal form in individual ones of its products, that is in finite spirits.

The first view is for the present time a useless curiosity. For us it would hardly be of any value *religiously*, that the Absolute has attained to personality at the conclusion of its development. On the contrary, an account of the way in which this result is reached is demanded by no religious need, but at the very most only by speculative curiosity.

The other view would be compelled to assert

that the Absolute, of itself unconscious and impersonal, produces even in its blind development the favoring conditions under which its own products, the finite spirits, developed the personality denied to itself. This is likewise an opinion that answers to no religious need; and least of all to the necessity of making intelligible from a single real principle, not merely the external course of the world, but also its moral order, and the fact that it furnishes us with obligatory ideals of the Good and the Holy.

In this way it is made apparent that very powerful motives impel the religious spirit, at last, straight to the conception of a *personal* God, and do not permit it to shrink back from the many difficulties that lie in this conception also.

CHAPTER III.

THE METAPHYSICAL ATTRIBUTES OF GOD.

§ **27.** We abandon the previous train of thought and now consider the conception of God as, on the basis of the incentives depicted in the last chapter, by means of a long spiritual labor of the centuries and essentially harmonious, it lies before us perfected in the monotheistic religions. We consider, first, the formal or metaphysical determinations.

That God is but *One*, and that polytheism is therefore excluded, we pass with a bare allusion. *Many* Gods, if each lived independent in his own world, would be a useless and adventurous thought; but if they met each other with their activity in one and the same world, then they would necessarily be finite beings, which acted on each other and suffered effects from each other in accordance with certain laws appointed over them.

The religious nature does not understand the 'Unity of God' in the aforesaid numerical meaning. It does not intend to affirm that God is in fact only one, while by way of imagination there might possibly be beside him still others of his own kind. It means rather that God is an *only* God; that is to say, there is no superior general concept of a God, of such sort that all the predicates which might belong to the actual God as an example of this concept of species, would ensue from it just as much conditioned and prescribed as in the case of every finite creature, from whose concept of species ensues the limit within which its properties and their reciprocal combination can vary.

This absolute independence of the Highest Principle, which does not admit of its being in any way subordinated to one still higher,—as though it were effect or even mere example of the latter,—will appear to us subsequently in the different consequences which are to be drawn from it, as one of the most important of the formal determinations.

§ 28. To a second formal predicate, that of Unchangeableness, the religious feeling does not attach the same meaning as seems to accord with this title.

Perfectly unchangeable substances would, of course, be philosophically useless assumptions even for the explanation of nature; but still, if one chooses to avoid certain questions as to first principles, such substances always admit of being employed for the intermediate explanation of processes one from the other. A God, on the contrary, who should be without changeable inner states forever perfectly self-identical, would answer to no religious need.

We need, in brief, a *living* God; and, therefore, by his 'unchangeableness' nothing further is meant than the consistency with which all these inner states proceed from a nature that remains the same. On this point we are in accord with Metaphysic also, which requires of the nature of all substances — even of such as are finite — only this consistent exclusiveness of the series of forms within which each being among them varies; it does not, however, require the monotony and rigidity of a perfect unchanging self-likeness.

§ 29. A third formal predicate, Omnipresence, seems only at first sight to ascribe to God an attribute of *spatiality* such as we otherwise impute merely to matter. The religious meaning of this expression signifies rather the opposite.

Concerning finite things we know that if they act upon each other immediately, it is only when in spatial contact, and therefore where they are;

on the contrary, if they act at a distance, it is only mediately (by means of the propagation of their first action to elements lying between): or we know that, if we concede to them an immediate action from afar, this action at least has its maximum when the nearness is greatest, and diminishes as the distance increases.

Both limitations are supposed not to be true of God. If he wills to act upon any element of the world, then his activity is supposed not to have to traverse any way, long or short, up to the point where such element exists. Conversely, if an element of the world—for example, a finite spirit with his prayer—wills to act upon God, then it is not necessary to traverse any way in order to discover God, as though he had a definite position in space. The rather is the activity of God everywhere alike immediately and perfectly present, without difference of degree.

Only this is meant by 'Omnipresence.' On the contrary, no one ever had any interest in ascribing positively to God himself, as one of his attributes, the predicate of an infinitely great extension in space. Quite the opposite, the simple design has been held of denying with reference to him in every respect that power to put under conditions which space-limitation exercises upon the reciprocal action of finite beings.

§ 30. The predicate of Omnipotence obviously presupposes that conceptions of activity, either barely transforming or else creative, have some applicability to God; and, under this presupposition, it is then sought to exalt the power of God absolutely above all bounds; but in the ordinary conception of this attribute such a result is not obtained.

The simplest interpretation of Omnipotence, that "God can do all possible," does not satisfy the religious feeling; we should thus obtain only the relatively greatest one of those finite forces which, collectively, are obliged to acknowledge certain limits of 'possibility' that stand fixed independently of them. God would therefore be subjected to a sphere of laws antecedent even to himself, which would determine for him the free scope of his power.

The other explanation — "God can make even the impossible to be possible and actual" — without doubt expresses the real heart-meaning of the religious feeling, but, in the aforesaid way of formulating it, appears absurd and unthinkable. For all order, all consistency and all coherency of the world appear to depend upon the limits between the possible and the impossible being absolutely immovable. If that which is of itself impossible can once be made possible by any power whatever, then every sure foundation for making any conclusion whatever in relation to the coherency of the world falls away.

But even this last explanation does the very thing for which it finds fault with the first; it assumes that this distinction of the impossible from the possible already exists independently of God. God finds them both already determined and authenticated by means of a truth that is independent of himself; and only *in practice* does the capacity belong to him of withdrawing aught that is subordinated to the self-authenticated conception of the impossible, from the domain of this conception, and of disposing it under the conception of the possible.

The thought mentioned above is neither sound in general, nor is such an omnipotence actually unlimited. Rather must we arrive at such an apprehension of God as makes God himself to be the prime reason for the opposition of the possible and the impossible having any significance at all in the world of actual existence.

This thought, which is hard to define in the present connection, we shall pursue further later on. For our immediate purpose, that which is of religious value in it permits of being most simply and effectively expressed in the not quite correct form that "God can do even the impossible." This form at least states one thing clearly,—to wit, that the impossible is no barrier for God.

§ 31. The predicate of Eternity in time depends upon different motives; first, as may be readily understood, upon the need that we be able to regard what is to be our support and our consolation as at no time ready to fail. But then, apart from every religious need, eternal duration is æsthetically an imposing idea on account of a sublimity which is worthy of the Absolute Principle.

But the aforesaid expression, nevertheless, does not itself depend upon our seeing any value or any advantage in the bare filling-up of infinite time. Just as we did not apprehend omnipresence as a positive magnitude in space, but only as the negation of all restrictive significations of space for the action of God; just so, 'infinite duration' signifies only the perfect independence of all those conditions that change in time, by which finite beings are constantly confined within a definite tract of their possible existence.

§ 32. Moreover 'Time' also, like Space, is not to be thought of as though it were a somehow self-existing form, and as though God had only the capacity of filling it up by his existence, however far it may extend. But the difficult attempts which have been made to apprehend this relation otherwise, — to consider time as in God, or God as above time, — we must defer provisionally and make prominent another point instead.

God, as filling eternal time in a perfectly unchangeable way, would be a mental representation of no service for religious interests. But if God is living and the subject of change, — that is, if anything whatever takes place within him, then it follows that he is in every second instant another than he was in the first instant preceding; — unless it can be demonstrated on other grounds in what way that 'Unity' of his Being which is for us indispensable is maintained continuously through the course of his changes in time.

Now, at this point we derive from Metaphysic the conviction that such 'Unity of a Being with itself' certainly presupposes all its successive states to be comprehensible as different consequences of one and the same nature, and — in brief — to cohere together in accordance with one and the same formula; but, likewise, the conviction that this presupposition is not at all adequate. For if *we* also, the thinking subjects, in the series of states $a, a_1, a_2, a_3, \ldots$, everywhere observe the secondary effect of the original nature a of a being; and if we, on this account, apprehend such a series as the history of one and the same being a: still it is in this way by no means yet proved, that this is more than a subjective apprehension on our part;—that is to say, that the $a, a_1, a_2, \ldots$, are not different successive beings instead of only successive states of one and the same Being (a).

If the latter conclusion is to be proved, then only the Being a itself can prove it; and, of course, only by itself doing what, previously, merely we, the investigating subjects, have done. The Being a must comprehend itself as a 'unity'; must, as such, set itself over against the series $a, a_1, \ldots$, as mere states of its own, and be able to unite these successive states into one synchronous state by means of recollection. Expressed in simple manner: In no respect can we assert of selfless 'Things,' but only of a self-conscious 'Spirit,' that it remains in the course of its history one and the same; and, for the very reason that only *it* actualizes the aforesaid unity by means of this deed of self-consciousness. Of a 'Thing,' on the contrary, —since it is merely subject to different states one after another, although in a sequence according to law, — there is no decisive test by which to prove the fact and the means of its distinguishing itself from a succession of different and merely related Things.

CHAPTER IV.

OF THE PERSONALITY OF THE ABSOLUTE.

§ **33**. The paradoxical result of the previous reflections is as follows: If all the predicates of 'unconditionateness' are to be valid for the Highest Being, then one condition of this validity lies precisely in the addition of a last formal predicate, — namely, that of Personal Existence.

At the faith in this 'personality of God' the religious faculty, naturally enough, has not arrived by the above-mentioned way, but from familiar motives that lie nearer at hand. Against this faith, however, philosophic reflection has subsequently been very unanimously directed with the assertion: 'Personality' is conceivable only in finite spirits, and in this case rests on conditions which can have no significance for the Absolute.

The above-mentioned investigations concerning the possibility or impossibility of the assumption of a 'personal God' should be briefly repeated in this connection.

§ **34**. Two thoughts which we believe ourselves obliged to distinguish, lie in the conception of 'personality.'

First: No 'personality,' or — what can for the moment pass as identical with it — no 'self-consciousness' is conceivable without our ascribing to the spiritual subject, to which it is to belong, an image of cognition or an image of representation, of that which this subject itself is, and by means of which it distinguishes itself from others. Since these images of cognition, as well as those which we project for ourselves from other objects, may be more or less either correct or false; therefore, self-consciousness is by no means identical with 'adequate self-cognition.' We are rather to estimate the different degrees of its clearness and perfection exactly according to the measure of the conformity of its content with the actual nature of the subject.

But the mental representation of the aforesaid picture will always deserve the title of 'self-consciousness' so long as it contains this second factor: — to wit, so long as the other additional thought is present, that this mental image is the image of *ourselves*, and is by no means distinguished from any other image merely in the same way that a second object is distinguished from a third; but that it is rather significant of somewhat which, as 'ego,' is to be placed in a fundamental and incomparable opposition to all else. This second transaction we consider in the first place.

§ 35. It is a very common opinion that 'self-consciousness' is a spiritual phenomenon which develops very gradually, and the origin and necessary conditions of which, accordingly, have a history.

Such an opinion we recognize as correct only in relation to the first of the points distinguished above. To wit: We doubtless do not arrive at the knowledge of the properties of which we compose the before-mentioned mental image, or at the content of the image of ourselves which we construct for ourselves, except by means of an accumulation of external and internal experiences.

But in relation to the other point we cannot assent to this opinion. It does not admit of being shown intelligibly, how, in the course of the projection of manifold mental representations, the moment must necessarily at some time arrive, when we should be compelled to consider one of these representations, not merely as image of one object which is distinguished from a second only in the same way as the latter from a third, but precisely as the image of our 'ego,' which stands in that absolute opposition to every non-ego, so easily intelligible but so difficult further to describe.

It will be found that the apparent 'origin' of self-consciousness in this sense always presupposes the latent previous existence of its most essential element, — namely, of a *self-feeling* in the same sense.

§ 36. The materialistic attempts to generate self-consciousness from all manner of motions in brain-atoms returning upon themselves, are deserving of no respect. As they are unable in general to deduce any 'consciousness' from motions, so is this return of the motions also unable to generate any *self*-consciousness.

But, on the whole, the frequent philosophical assertions — Personality can only be generated by an activity of the ego proceeding outward, and by a resistance of the non-ego which 'reflects' this activity upon its own point of issue — are not a whit better. These modes of speech correspond to absolutely no demonstrable and real transaction. Such an activity of the ego proceeding outward nowhere admits of being designated by name. The analogy that it is thrown back like rays of light from the non-ego, is a mental image utterly without real *motif*, and one under which it is not possible to bring any actual procedure. The conclusion finally, that this activity becomes 'self-consciousness' by means of such 'reflection,' is a bare subreption. For it is precisely by this means that the mere return of the activity to its own point of issue is occasioned. But that it should now be compelled to apprehend this point as its own self, — and hence the precise origin of self-consciousness, — is a mere supplement of thought devoid of all basis.

Only those attempts would deserve consideration which aim to show how the soul originally produces merely intuitive ideas, and then, in the course of the reciprocal actions of these its individual products, projects also conceptions of non-intuitive subjects to which the aforesaid ideas belong as predicates; that it finally succeeds also in assigning by thought one subject to the totality of all its inner states; and that it thus generates the consciousness of the 'ego' as of that one which is at the same time subject and object of the act of ideation.

§ 37. It is to be alleged, in the first place, against such attempts as the foregoing, that identity of ideating subject and ideated object is the general notion of every personality; and that, therefore, 'I' is not by this means distinguishable from 'thou' and 'he.' And yet 'self-consciousness' or 'personality' obviously does not consist in subsuming ourselves, together with all others under one and the same general notion : but it consists in our *distinguishing* ourselves from all others within this general notion.

It might now be said: 'I' am subject and object of my thoughts, 'thou' art subject and object of thine, etc. If distinguishing thus is not to bring us round and round in a constant circle, then the distinction between 'mine' and 'thine' — the one we need to make — cannot be deduced from the fact that the 'mine' belongs to the 'I,' and the 'thine' to the 'thou'; but between both of them there must already exist a distinction that is absolutely clear, immediately given, and in need of no deduction at all.

Such now is actually the case; and the distinction depends upon this, that we are in general unable to think of any soul exclusively as a being active merely in the formation of ideas. Every soul is rather likewise capable of experiencing feelings of pleasure and of pain, and of combining these feelings with the content of ideas. Simply by means of the fact that the idea of any state whatsoever is combined with a feeling of pleasure or pain, is such state authenticated as *our own*, and no longer passes merely as the state of *some* being or other.

We express the matter simply by means of the following antithesis: Granted that some superior spirit possesses so perfect an intelligence as to have a quite adequate cognition of all things, and of its own being as well, and yet is utterly lacking in the faculty for pleasure and pain; and that every conceivable content is therefore as indifferent to it as is every other. Then such a spirit will not merely cognize itself, but will also know that in this case the cognizing subject is identical with the object cognized. It will, however, at the same time cognize the fact, that the case of such identity may occur precisely so millions of times in other beings; and it will have no motive at all to regard one of these cases — just that one which occurs in its own self — as something special, and to distinguish this case from those others; it will not, therefore, apprehend itself as an 'ego' set over against some other as the 'non-ego.' On the other hand, an animal of the lowest order, that has scarcely any cognition of itself at all, but has indeed feeling for pleasure and pain, will never confound itself with the external world. When it feels a smart, it will experience this state as one belonging to itself alone; and just by this means will it feel itself as an 'ego' in opposition to the whole world, although it would not know at all how to specify precisely in what its own being consists.

§ 38. We arrive at the same goal by another way. We often hear it said: 'Ego' and 'non-ego' are two correlative conceptions, neither of which has in general any significance apart from its opposition to the other. Therefore, — it is said, — even the idea of the 'ego' can originate only at the moment when that of the 'non-ego' likewise originates. On this account, 'personality' is possible only for finite beings which can be limited by a non-ego.

The foregoing three propositions have really no inner connection with each other. The first of them must be pronounced perfectly absurd. Two conceptions, each of which should have a meaning *only* as a negation of the other, and should signify nothing further, would both of them have no meaning at all, and would not even acquire any by their being opposed to each other. One of the two must necessarily be independently determined and signify something.

On consideration of our case we find the question to be: If 'ego' and 'non-ego' were two such conceptions, each of which contained barely the negation of the other: by what means would the soul then be induced, at the moment of the simultaneous origin of both, to rank itself under the conception of the 'ego' rather than under that of the 'non-ego'; and what does it gain thereby if it does the one and forbears the other? To such a question no answer is possible but just this; that one of the two conceptions signifies somewhat independently determined, and on this account the spirit applies it to itself, or does not so apply it. Now, without going further, the expressions themselves show that this independent significance belongs only to the 'ego' as positively apprehended. What is meant by the term is directly obvious: what, on the contrary, is meant by the negative expression 'non-ego' is in a preliminary way obscure; and only thus much is known about it, — namely, that it is *not* the 'ego.'

But this is just what would be achieved by the aforesaid immediate feeling, by which the ego positively apprehends what belongs to it as *its own;* and, on the other hand, at first excludes from 'itself' in a merely negative way what does not belong to it.

§ 39. The above position being conceded, it is still always possible to say: This 'feeling of the ego,' although in itself of a definite content, which does not primarily originate by means of its opposition to the non-ego, nevertheless, as a matter of fact, cannot actually occur except at the moment of such an opposition. To see colors is also an original capacity of the soul, and could not be procured for it by means of any waves of ether, if it did not of itself possess the capacity; yet we do see colors solely in case waves of ether act on us. Just so we feel ourselves as 'ego,' only in case an opposed non-ego acts on us.

On this point it is now to be observed, that the possibility of personality is in any case erroneously attached to the opposition to a *real* non-ego; as though by means of it that being, which in consequence thereof then feels itself as 'ego,' became really limited.

A reciprocal action with a real non-ego, of such kind that this *as such* might enter into consciousness and the ego thus be posited in opposition to this perceived non-ego, never occurs at all. In all sensations and perceptions, what enters consciousness in consequence of such an influence, is invariably nothing but some inner state belonging to the spiritual being, — the sensation or mental representation itself; it is never the reality by means of which the state is brought about.

From these inner states the entire subsequent development of the spiritual life, and therefore that of the personality, proceeds. It suffices for laying the foundation of the latter, if a spiritual being has the faculty of apprehending itself as 'I' in opposition to its own states, which are only its 'states' and not 'I.' A relation to an external reality is not necessary; and, consequently, 'personality' also is not bound to the condition of *finiteness*, — to wit, to that of being limited by another reality of the same kind.

§ 40. It may nevertheless always be said: Even if, in a course of thought that is once in process, this world of thoughts can serve as the non-ego in opposition to which the thinking spirit knows itself as the ego, still the first excitation of such process of thought needs the influence from without which can only be given by an actual reality affecting the senses. But this objection unwarrantably carries over what takes place as a matter of fact in the case of us men, as though it were indispensable to every personality.

In all attempts at a physical explanation of the world, we are at last under the necessity of recognizing, not merely certain real elements, but also certain motions of the same, as original *data;* and it is of no advantage to search further for the causes of these motions also, — since they could only consist of still other motions; nor is it conceivable how we are ever to get from a state of equilibrium or rest as originally assumed, to disturbance of equilibrium or to motion.

Only the same concession, and no more, is required in relation to the Infinite Spirit. It is not to be thought of as somewhat which it were barely possible to imagine, but as somewhat which is imagined as eternally and unceasingly actual; — somewhat to which no such state of rest was ever antecedent, as a state from which it would have been obliged to be extricated by means of special influence.

§ 41. All further inquiries concerning this matter (as to what, perhaps, gives conditions to this eternal movement of thought with respect to its content and its direction) must, of course, remain unanswered. Nevertheless it can be shown — not, indeed, with a strictness that satisfies the demands of science, but still in a manner intelligible to imagination, — why the matter stands with us men in that different fashion which we should not be justified in wanting to carry over and apply to God.

When treating of 'Omnipresence' allusion was made to the truth, that God, who is the truly Existent in all Things and comprises them all as mere modifications of his Being, stands in need of no mediation through transmitted effects, in order to be acquainted with the individual elements of the world and the states belonging to them. Every finite spirit, however, has its existence only from a definite point of time onward, and has in the coherence of all Things a determinate position in the system, which assigns to it also a limited place in space.

Now it follows from the above-mentioned truth, that finite spirits, who have very much outside of themselves which they themselves *are not*, stand in absolute need of a real outside world and of its effects, in order to attain to the development of the life of thought possible to them.

It is intelligible, further, that finite spirits who are not the Absolute itself but only modifications or fragments of the same, and yet likewise possess all their existence only through this Absolute, do constantly, in case they reflect upon themselves, suppose that they find an obscure germ in their own being, — to wit, just this power of the Absolute itself. This power it is which works through and through them, and, without their own assistance, prescribes for them the universal forms of their spiritual activity, their sensation, imagination, judgment, etc.; and which permits them only within narrow limits to dispose further of this dowry, and to pursue their special ends. That is to say, therefore: 'Personality' is in *them* only very imperfectly accomplished. There remains something back in the ego, which it cannot itself explain. This is a fact which is corroborated by the course of Psychology, wherein always at last the question recurs, — What then really are we? and can never be answered to our perfect satisfaction.

Finally, it does not indeed admit of direct proof, but is none the less a probable assumption, that the laws of the psychical mechanism to which our inner life is subjected are also connected with this 'finiteness.' From them it follows, however, that our ideas inhibit one another; that only a small number of them is at any time present in consciousness; that the forgotten ones return, indeed, to our recollection in accordance with general laws, but not always in a manner corresponding to our momentary need. Hence it comes about that we frequently over-hasten ; that we permit certain measures of conception which are just present in consciousness, partially to pass over into transactions which we later, when we have collected ourselves, may no longer recognize as our own ; that, finally, we forget very much, and with increasing age can no longer transport ourselves back into the frames of mind, feelings and enthusiasms of the earlier epochs of life.

All these hindrances of a perfect 'personality' we can imagine as not existent in the Infinite Spirit. On this account, we conclude with the assertion which is exactly the opposite of the customary one: *Perfect* personality is compatible only with the conception of an Infinite Being; for finite beings only an approximation to this is attainable.

CHAPTER V.

OF THE CONCEPTION OF CREATION.

§ 42. We reserve the further concrete predicates, chiefly of an ethical kind, by which we have to complete the still abstract conception of an infinite personality, until after we have considered the relation of this personality to the world. And this relation itself we treat for convenience under the three distinctive names of Creation, Preservation and Government.

In relation to the first topic, we omit all ancient and modern cosmogonies, such as intend to furnish an intuitive picture of the process of 'creation' and of the succession of particular creative acts; — a picture, which is in general impossible, and in particulars not to be established with any certainty. Our design is merely to show what fundamental conceptions admit of being formed concerning that relation of God to the world from which the creation proceeds, or in which it consists, or which is established by means of it.

We divide the essentially different views, which are possible on this subject, into the three following: the first of which attempts to trace the world to the "consistent development of the nature of God," the second to his will, the third to a creative act.

§ 43. The first view, crudely elaborated and satisfying merely to the imagination but not to speculation, appears in all the emanation theories of ancient and modern times. This we exclude from our investigation.

On the contrary, the conception of the world as a 'necessary, involuntary, and inevitable development of the nature of God,' which rests essentially upon the foundation of modern scientific views, is worthy of consideration.

So far as this view endeavors to exclude a God who rules without principle in blind arbitrariness, it is correct; and in this respect corresponds also to our religious need. But we must resist with the greatest possible decisiveness the further apotheosis of the notion of 'development' consequent upon this view, which it is customary just now to express and to extol with such great emphasis, as though it were identical, as a matter of course, with all that is great and sublime and holy.

If it were only a question concerning a theoretic explanation of the course of the world, then such a conception would be satisfactory. But it is wholly useless from the religious point of view, because it leads consistently to nothing but a thorough-going Determinism, according to which not only is every thing that must happen, in case certain conditions occur, appointed in pursuance of general laws; but according to which even the successive occurrence of these conditions, and consequently the whole of history with all its details, is predetermined.

In such a mechanical contrivance there is no place whatever for any 'freedom' or 'activity,' or for an effort that shall produce aught which does not originate from the mechanism itself. Religious opinion assumes rather that, while there are universal laws, without whose efficacy no 'design' whatever would be able by definite means to attain to a definite goal, there is however at the same time, on the basis and in the domain of this reign of law, a free, voluntary activity, which, by the use and combination of the given elements acting in accordance with law, produces that even, which would have no existence without such activity.

The above-mentioned assumption has its difficulties. Until, however, it is shown decisively to be impossible, the religious feeling will never return to the thought of an 'undesigned, inevitable development' of the world from the nature of God, but will derive it from an act of the divine will, *without* which it would not have existed.

§ 44. In speaking of the will of God, we naturally think first of the analogy of our own will; we may not however summarily transfer to the former that which is peculiar to the latter.

Now the aims to which our will can be directed, are only given to us finite beings progressively by means of experience. Hence under the term 'will' we conceive primarily of a spiritual activity momentarily awakening, which is directed chiefly to the production of a state not yet existing, or to the change of a state already existing. Even in those cases in which we 'will' nothing new but merely the *status quo*, we become conscious of this act of will, at least distinctly so, only if something threatens to disturb this state that has been 'willed' by us.

The foregoing conceptions are not applicable to the creative will of God. Although the imagination naturally represents the dependence of the world upon the will of God in the most forcible manner by making a period of time precede in which even this creative will of God had no existence; still there is no ground whatever for forming a philosophical tenet out of this view,

— harmless as it is to religion, — and for speaking of an inner life in God, which, after this period, has proceeded to the decision to create and to its execution. Besides it would be impossible to fill this space of time with anything but a delusive history of development, in which the systematic coherence of all the thoughts, by uniting which we endeavor to interpret for ourselves the being of God, would be fictitiously converted into a chronological sequence; and by this means the nature of God would for the first time become completely realized.

This is, philosophically considered, erroneous, and religiously devoid of all significance: we abide therefore by the assumption, that the 'will to create' is an absolutely eternal predicate of God, and ought not to be used to designate a deed of his so much as the absolute dependence of the world upon his will in contradistinction to its involuntary 'emanation' from his nature.

§ 45. With the foregoing assertion, however, there seems to vanish something which we regard as necessary for the religious conception of creation; to wit, a will which is constantly existent, has no longer the character of a *deed*. In order that will may be distinguished from that involuntary development, from which we intended to distinguish it, it seems necessary that some *deed* or *work* be added to the act of will, by whose accomplishment alone that which is willed truly becomes the complete possession of the one who wills, and at the same time becomes a reality. There is involved herein an undoubtedly genuine religious need, but it is wrongly formulated in dependence upon analogies derived from our own willing and doing, which are not transferable to God.

In the first place as regards the efficacy of our own will, we know psychologically that our 'willing' can never do anything else but produce a definite psychical state within us (an idea, a feeling, a wish). With this state, as soon as it is once in existence, an order of nature under the control of general law, wholly independent of our volition and hardly accessible to our intelligence, has connected a definite result; and this result then originates without our being able to comprehend the process of its origination or to contribute anything further to it.

Now we believe to be sure that, in the performance of our corporal movements, we feel at once the transition of our will to the limbs, and that to a certain extent we observe the will at its work, by which it brings to pass the effect. But it is known psychologically, that we actually feel in this case only the changes, which the will, in a manner wholly beyond the power of observation, has already produced in the limbs, and from which, in a supplemental way, the sensations of weariness and exertion are produced in the consciousness. These feelings therefore do not show us how those movements are produced by us; but they only show how much disturbance our organism has experienced, in consequence of those movements having been attached to the action of our will, in accordance with an order of nature unknown to us.

If therefore we recognize as our own 'deed' an effect which issues from us only in case we have had, at the time of its accomplishment, all the aforesaid feelings, then this analogy of the human will cannot be transferred to God. For this apparent activity in accomplishing something beyond the bare action of willing is in truth merely a witness to the powerlessness of our will, which effects something only in case a higher power has united with it the origination of changes in external objects.

In this sense, therefore, we may not, in addition to the creative will of God, still further postulate a special creative deed; but we must be satisfied with the thought that the will of the Supreme Being is without further procedure the realization of that which He wills.

§ 46. But after all there remains a genuine religious need, which was expressed, although wrongly, by the demand for a divine *work* of creation.

The value of the feelings, to which we referred, does not consist in the fact that they brought to our view the *modus agendi* of our will, but that at each minutest instant they furnished us the knowledge as to how far the realization of its activity had already advanced. Suppose, for example, that we give our arm a wide swing, then we have at each minutest point of time a new sensation which discloses to us the magnitude of the breadth of the movement already executed; and therefore the progress of our wills' mode of operation, although in itself unobserved, is noted by us from the beginning to the end of the movement. Now it is precisely because in such a case our consciousness always has an immediate feeling in conjunction with the product of the will, that such movements appear as, in the strictest sense, our own living deed. On the contrary, in the case of the stone that flies away from the hand at the completion of that movement of the arm, although it has in fact got its velocity by means of us, still we have no immediate sensation of its further movement. While this movement, therefore, as well as its subsequent effects upon other objects, seem to us to be consequences of our deed, they no longer seem to be our own activity itself.

Now it is the counterpart of just this, which it is really intended to exclude from the conception of the divine creative work. It is not to be supposed that the act of will originates a bare result in which the consciousness of the one who wills were no longer present; but it is to be supposed that the creative will remains in that constant feeling in conjunction with the state of its product, which we men experience only on occasion of the movements of our own body, and not on occasion of the movements of external objects indirectly produced.

Now because this feeling in our case is psychologically connected with the effort and labor, which are simply a consequence of our finite nature, some have arrived at the false conception that this must be so even in the case of God Himself; and on this account have demanded the aforesaid special *work* of creation.

§ 47. The sum and substance of the preceding discussion is, that the conception of creation properly signifies nothing more than this; that the world, with respect to its existence as well as its content, is completely dependent upon the will of God, and not a mere involuntary 'development' of his nature; that it proceeds, however, only from the will and not from a special work of God, — this latter conception being always applicable only in cases where a will endeavors to realize its purpose in conflict with an existing world that is independent of it: whereas of God we in fact assert that He "has created the world out of nothing," — a strange expression, which strictly interpreted means to say, in a merely negative manner, that there is nothing out of which God constructed the world; and which then whimsically makes this Nothing appear again as a sort of 'stuff' from which it is created.

There can be no consistent description of the process of creation, for the reason that there is no such process. Such process in fact, whenever the attempt has been made to imagine it, has always presupposed in turn the existence of another world, and of certain forms of happening already in use in it.

In regard still further to the content of creation, it would be from a religious point of view an object of interest for us, only in case we conceive withal of a plan which is to be realized in the world ; and this subject is to be discussed under the head of the conception of 'Government.'

CHAPTER VI.

OF PRESERVATION.

§ 48. To ascribe the preservation of the world to a special divine activity, may seem to be a superfluous thought. In fact, the common opinion of natural philosophy amounts to this, that the world, when once in existence, maintains itself as a matter of course by the efficacy of the laws which have once gained prevalence in it. The utmost that is conceded is, that the origination of the world may be the object of an action, but not its continuation after it has once originated.

The foregoing opinion only serves to remind us that we really have already before us, even with respect to creation, a difficulty of which, in the ordinary reflection, we are less sensible only in relation to this conception of preservation. To wit, the question is raised, in what way God, in the action of his will, has arrived at a decision concerning that which should be or should not be.

The readiest answer, — namely that He has summoned into actual existence only that which is in itself possible, — as well as the other answer, — that He has summoned into actual existence the best among many possible worlds, both contain the thought that what is good or not good, possible or not possible, has already been decided independently of the will of God; and therefore that, after all, there precedes God, the Supreme Principle, a certain realm of eternal truths as a still higher Principle, to which He together with his activity is now obliged to become subordinate.

This strange idea is not improved by the immediate reply that, in the use of a distinction frequently made, we designate those 'eternal truths' merely as the 'content of God's understanding,' and not as a necessity foreign to Him and which stands over against Him objectively. No improvement of the idea is attained so long at least as we have in mind in this connection our own spiritual life, in which of course all these general truths appear as something proceeding from a higher power and not connected with our personality; or, at all events, as something not deducible from it.

Concerning these difficulties we must make the following somewhat detailed reflections.

§ 49. It has already been observed, in discoursing of the possibility of the reciprocal actions of the elements of the world, that the prevalent method of speaking of the "authority of general laws of nature over Things" has nothing properly corresponding to it in the actual state of the case.

Laws can exist only in a twofold manner: they may either exist at the instant when they are obeyed, as the activity of the elements themselves, which seem to follow them; or, in the observing spirits which compare the events, as conscious rules for the combination of the ideas, by which we (the observing spirits) are enabled, in accordance with the reality, to determine beforehand from given states those which succeed them.

On the contrary, laws never exist *outside*, *between*, *beside*, or *above* the Things that are to obey them. And if we ourselves should intend to assume that a ghost-like existence, of a sort that is wholly beyond the power of representation, belongs to them, the question would be left the more unanswerable, how in that case they went to work to secure obedience from the elements which were wholly foreign to them.

This first mode of representation, then, according to which God even would have 'found at hand' a sum of self-existing truths, must be wholly abandoned.

§ 50. The first modification of the thought we are considering, to the effect that the eternal truths were nothing else but the mode of the action of God's own nature and intelligence, we found, just at the close of the last paragraph but one, to be not altogether satisfactory.

To wit: we find in ourselves such truths (as for example the law of identity, or the simple geometrical intuitions, or the fundamental ethical judgments of our conscience), as do not present themselves to us, at any rate when considered *individually*, as something foreign to our nature, but as the mode of our own experience or the form of our own activity. But we find *several* of such truths within us, and we find no connection between them. For, from the fact that the proposition of identity is a necessity of our thought, it by no means certainly follows that we must also have an intuition of space, or must make a distinction between good and evil. Hence the aggregate of these truths seems to us after all to be something foreign to our own being, and not deducible from it; or at least something whose origin from it cannot be known.

If it were thus with God, it would seem to us as if He met with these eternal truths, not to be sure as forces external to Himself, but as something within Himself, which He could regard only in the light of a gift bestowed upon Him as it were.

Now we can of course never give a positive description of the manner in which those truths, that to our discernment are disparate, are united with each other in God, and are experienced as belonging together in the unity of a single thought. But, for all that, there is no contradiction in the assumption that with God it is so; and that only we finite beings, who are able to possess nothing but fragments of the whole of truth, fail to grasp the inner connection by which these truths are perfected into one whole.

§ 51. The above-mentioned view of the case also often proves unsatisfactory. The assumption, that the eternal truths are the proper *modus agendi* of the divine understanding itself, has always seemed to many to involve after all a limitation of his unconditionateness and omnipotence. In such case we should not be content with anything less than the statement that God did not *possess* this *modus agendi*, but that He first *bestowed* it upon Himself. Indeed even in such case it might perhaps still be doubted, whether in the choice of such a *modus* from among many that are conceivable and now excluded, there were not after all again involved a limitation of his unconditionateness, although a self-chosen limitation.

In one view of the matter, however, it may be remarked that in this way the conception of God loses all content whatever; and that, instead of conceiving of that concrete Being to whom unconditionateness in respect to his conduct belongs, we have made the empty conception of unconditionateness itself the subject or the principle of the world. To do this is, fundamentally considered, just the same mistake that is made when we content ourselves with the abstract expressions, the 'One,' the 'Existent,' the 'Absolute,' etc., and suppose that by them we have expressed the Supreme Principle, instead of designating by name or representing that which deserves to be acknowledged as the Real Principle of the world, because it possesses in virtue of its own concrete nature the alleged predicates.

But the misunderstandings that arise in this connection admit of being analyzed somewhat further in detail.

§ 52. If, in the first place, we see a limitation of omnipotence in the fact, that even omnipotence, from its very beginning onward, follows a definite *modus agendi*, then we may in the next place be reminded that we in fact never mentally represent even any finite 'power' or 'capacity' as a predicate which would inhere in a Thing without connection with its remaining n predicates as an $(n+1)$th. Just as little do we represent such a power as a 'being able in general,' which would still have no direction whatever; so that it would only be determined subsequently by secondary circumstances, what sort of activity this 'being able' will exercise, and with reference to what objects.

On the contrary every 'power' or 'capacity' is conceivable only as one that is quite definitely fixed in reality. And the abstract conception of 'capacity in general,' which we may form just as legitimately as the conception of 'motion in general,' can just as little signify something real as can the latter before it is again furnished with a 'direction' and a 'velocity,' from which, in the formation of the general conception, the abstraction was made.

If now this conception of 'power' is to be exalted to that of 'omnipotence,' it cannot be accomplished by omitting every such act of determination as would fix some *modus agendi;* but only by representing just this *modus* as one so comprehensive, that all actual capacities and powers whatever, which appear in the world, originate from it. In that, we should have substituted the mere general conception of power for the supreme actual Power. But still further, omnipotence, even in this case, cannot be conceived of as a predicate additional to the rest of the predicates of God; but it is only an expression for the efficacy in action of just these predicates, and therefore of that concrete nature of God in which all reality is comprehended.

§ 53. We may now be tempted for the last time to inquire: If God's omnipotence is only co-extensive with his nature, why then has God this determinate nature a and not another b or c? and does not the fact that He is not this b or c involve again a limitation of his being?

In support of such thoughts an appeal is also made perhaps to the celebrated proposition "*Omnis determinatio est negatio*"; the meaning of which is often enough thought to be, that all determination is limitation, because it is the product of the negation of innumerable other possibilities.

Thus understood, the proposition would be thoroughly false. It is only in cases where a completely disjunctive judgment is already validated, in accordance with which a subject s must be either a or b or c, that the affirmation of a can originate from the negation of b and c. And even in such cases this negation is nothing more than a reason for our cognition, from which we *conclude* that s is a, but is not a reason in reality why s *is* actually a. That is to say; It is not the real determination, but our subjective certainty of its existence, that follows from the negation of other possibilities.

But in other cases, as a rule, the above-mentioned proposition can only signify, not that every determination originates from a negation of that which is different from it, but that it is accessory to, or consequent upon, such negation.

If we thus apprehend the proposition, the doubt above suggested will subside; the doubt, namely, whether after all there is not again involved a limitation of a, in the very fact that something can now no longer be b or c, because it is originally a. This thought has some significance for us finite beings, to whom a determinate nature α is given, beside and outside of which the natures β and γ of other beings — as for example those of other species of animals — are likewise met with as actualities. Since then we are unable to transpose ourselves out of our own nature into the β and γ foreign to us, this incapacity seems to us a limitation which prevents our enjoyment of a good that actually exists.

But the foregoing analogy is not transferable to the nature of God. For *this* nature a is precisely such an one as is not the product of a still higher nature M, among the consequences of which it would find itself coördinated with the other equally real products b and c: and at the same time excluded from them. But outside of this a nothing exists: a is rather the primal source of the sum-total of reality; and, indeed, a source of such sort that, owing to its concrete nature, thinking beings also are met with in this realm of reality, who are able to distinguish a from a never-existent, but conceivable non-a; and who now are able to raise the wondrous question, why all the world bears the character of this a and not the other character of a non-a.

The noteworthy capacity for denying in thought what actually exists, — a capacity which is itself only a product of the laws that are valid in actuality upon the basis of that a, — misleads us into the acceptance of this strange and utterly unthinkable idea: before God was and before the world was, there was already a multitude of coördinate, possible future Gods and worlds; and there was possible and necessary a choice between them, by which the total character a of the actual God, and of the actual World was established; but at the same time there was by this means introduced a limitation of both of them, because now they could no longer be b and c.

§ 54. We arrive at the same result, if we undertake to think through one of the two following propositions: 'God has only recognized the truth'; or, 'He has created it.'

Arbitrary statutes admit of being 'recognized' in so far as our transactions are willingly or reluctantly accommodated to them. But in thinking we can only 'recognize' as truth that which accords with the laws of such thinking,—that is, with its *modus agendi*. And thus even God would have been able to 'recognize' any 'truth' that he met with, as *truth*, only because it had already belonged to the intrinsic nature of his own thought.

Moreover statutes of all sorts admit of being 'made,' and a practical obedience to them may be enforced: but to *make* something which, after it is done, should constitute a truth, is only possible in case the productive energy itself is already of itself fulfilling, as rules of its own action, precisely the same conditions as those that are conditions of the truth to the intelligence associated with the energy.

By both paths, then, we return to the proposition, that eternal truths are neither antecedent norms nor subsequent products of the divine activity; but are nothing else than the actual form of this very energizing; and that, in the special sense of the word 'truth,' they appear as commands, which something not yet existent must satisfy, only in our subjective reflection, in case we attempt to bring the future into combination with the present.

§ 55. The foregoing considerations are connected with the conception of the Preservation of the world in the following manner.

The common view of nature, in modern times, either asserts that God indeed created the world at the beginning, but after it was created left it to itself and to the further development of the general laws which He established in it. Or, in the other case, since the act of creation can never be made apprehensible, such act is entirely left out; and it is simply asserted that the world which lies ready-made before us, is maintained by the constant prevalence of its general laws, and needs no divine support.

In opposition to this the proposition of religion is heard: "Preservation is continual new-creation."

It is not conceivable that this can be intended to mean: The world of the next instant is, as to its content, entirely new and foreign to that of the preceding instant. So far from this, we naturally accept the assumption that, in the divine activity, there is unity and coherence; and, for this reason, the creative act of the next instant also is a consequence of that of the preceding. But, nevertheless, the aforesaid proposition would deny that the world of one instant perpetuates itself by its own agency and by its general laws into the next instant.

For that very reason it will be superfluous, as regards all *special* inquiries into the coherence of the processes of nature, to come back to the 'co-working of God'; and it is sufficient to speak of the consecutive order of nature which He has established. Still, in our idea of the *whole*, we must decidedly guard against the view which speaks of an actual self-sufficiency of nature, and which, from this as from a secure stand-point, exercises a negative criticism in opposition to the religious intuitions.

It must rather be asserted that if corporal 'substance' is indestructible, it is not so by its own agency or in accordance with a claim to the right growing out of its own nature, but because the divine creative power preserves it continuously at each instant; and that if, in the course of nature, the same forces always act according to the same laws, this does not come to pass because these forces were of themselves eternal and these laws of themselves efficient, but because it lies within the plan of the divine efficiency to employ, at each instant of the course of the world, this number of homogeneous actions, as means for the production of more composite products.

In a word: The entire interior consistency of the cohering order of nature, upon which the natural sciences are supported, is conceded as a matter of fact; but taken as a whole and at large it is regarded as a system of mutually conditioning actualities, utterly dependent upon the divine power; so that ultimately, therefore, the World does not preserve itself but is preserved by God.

CHAPTER VII.

OF GOVERNMENT.

§ 56. We can only speak of Government in case there are elements that, with a certain independence of behavior on their part, threaten to withdraw from a plan prescribed to them, which the governing principle intends to realize.

The considerations to which we last referred therefore seem to leave no place for the application of this conception. Indeed, in proportion as these considerations themselves make the preservation of the world dependent upon the constant action of the will of God, do they obscure the thought to which we would firmly hold;—namely, that the World is not a mere immanent development of God, but a product of his will.

In order that this contradiction may have any significance, the product of the will, after it is created, would have to possess a certain independence. Or, to use a well-known mode of expression, the world would have to be 'outside' of God and not merely a process 'in' Him.

We need not adhere to these last mentioned expressions in terms of space which would lead to such endless and perfectly empty disputes; but the inquiry must be made as to what must really constitute that 'mode of behavior' which it is supposed may be figuratively designated by these expressions. And to this question the only answer will probably be, that only that Reality possesses the independence obviously here intended, which is able to have its *own states*, — such, that is, as are not immediately states of the 'Universal Substance'; and to initiate processes which do not proceed from that Substance.

If now we consider how these abstract postulates might be fulfilled, we find but one Reality which actually fulfils them; namely, spiritual life.

A being which has experience of itself as an individual subject for its own states, and which distinguishes these states from those of other beings, may, it is true, be nothing whatever as to its entire existence but a product of the Infinite Being. But after it is once in existence, it is, by the very form of its existence, by this consciousness which places itself in relation to itself, distinguished as an individual ego from the very Absolute, that in reality conditions it, and that now, as posited over against itself, belongs to the non-ego. And by this act, or by this form of its **existence**, does it possess that relative independence which we designate when we say that it is 'outside' of God.

§ 57. Hence it would follow (what we now remark only incidentally) that, with respect to our entire view of the World, we find ourselves in the presence of an alternative.

If spiritual life is the only form in which we can conceive of a reality that is not a mere state of some other real being, then our current idea of a motionless, blind and lifeless 'stuff,' which should exist outside of us, can signify nothing that is actual.

We must either assume, as the Idealist does, that what we regard as such a 'stuff' has no existence external to spirits, but that the self-coherent semblance of such a 'world-stuff' (compare especially J. G. Fichte), is merely produced within these spirits, and for them only, by a universal power which works in all spirits. Or else we must conclude, in entire agreement with the Spiritualists, that each atom of that which appears to us as mere 'stuff,' is after all something better than this; that is to say, it participates in the most general characteristic of the spiritual life: and this characteristic consists in somehow (either in distinct consciousness or in the mere feeling of pleasure and pain) '*being for self,*' and not in merely forming an object of contemplation for others.

It is only the common realistic opinion on this subject that would seem to us impossible, according to which an entirely 'selfless stuff' would be just as actually existent outside of us as we are wont commonly to represent it.

There is no doubt that either of the two foregoing views may be formed into an entirely consistent apprehension of the world. But from the religious point of view, we are not necessarily required to choose between them.

§ 58. If however there were in existence nothing more than an indefinite number of such independent, created beings, there would still be no foundation for the conception of a government of the world. It would still be thinkable, that the world might develop itself in a perfectly imperturbable harmony; and the problem for all spirits would consist in merely looking on, and in consciously and admiringly rejoicing in this fact.

In point of fact, however, religious sentiment has never been satisfied with this, but has always insisted, at the outset very obscurely although vigorously, that something new also must happen in the world, — something that is not a mere consequence of what has gone before ; — and that there must exist in individual spirits just this capacity to initiate a new series of events ; and therefore in brief a freedom of acting or primarily of willing, by which they separate themselves from the Universal Substance in a still more decided manner than by their mere 'Being for self' as relatively independent beings.

In this way then has the problem originated which leads to the conception of a government. For only after this is there any possibility of events by which the continuous realization of a predeterminate plan of the world might be interrupted.

§ 59. Even the above-mentioned demand for freedom would have no religious significance, if it were directed in a merely formal way to the possibility of new beginnings. For that something new happen in the world, has of itself no more value than that the whole course of the world be an uninterrupted, consecutive process of development ; in which of itself also, as we have already previously suggested, there is involved nothing that is worthy of adoration.

But we know surely, that we only demand this

formal 'freedom' because we regard it as the *conditio sine qua non* for the fulfilment of ethical commands, whose obligatory majesty we consider to be the most absolute certainty and one that needs no derivation from any other source whatever.

This conviction is the absolutely fundamental point upon which the entire religious character of our view of the world depends. And for him who does not directly experience and acknowledge this, all questions of religious philosophy are altogether superfluous.

§ 60. The ideas of freedom are not induced by speculation; but they rest entirely upon the fact of that penitence and self-condemnation in which we believe we find the immediate assurance of the possibility, that the choice, whose failure is now repented of, might have been reached even sooner than it was.

This idea is, in an obscure way, the first and most natural, the one that has precedence in human culture. It was not till a later period that the scientific contemplation of nature disclosed the conception of a 'necessary causal connection,' and then extended it over the whole course of the world, so that now the idea of freedom seems like a strange exception and as such is denied. It is acknowledged that even the ethical ideals originate in the mechanical course of psychical development. But how much influence they have upon our action, depends entirely upon the involuntary states and movements within our own interior being. It is therefore due to a process of nature, that the impulse to good actions, or even to bad actions, preponderates within us; and the mechanical conditions for such result may be strengthened by a correct or by a perverted education. But, to be consistent and candid about it, an action in the proper sense, such as would issue from our own ego, will then no longer exist. And even the inducement to all such reflection — that is, the feeling of penitence — will be regarded as a disagreeable state, about like a feeling of sickness; and it will be maintained that the wish involved in this feeling, — the wish that one had acted differently, — gives no assurance whatever of this having been possible at an earlier moment.

Such views as the foregoing are not to be got at by speculation; they involve no contradiction of cognition. If they are abandoned, it can be done only upon the basis of an undemonstrable *belief*, that after all there is directly disclosed in the aforesaid self-condemnation, the possibility of a free choice, without which 'the bad conscience' and the pain of 'penitence' would continue to be totally inexplicable phenomena in a rational order of the world.

§ 61. We cannot think of doing more than refute the objections against the possibility of the conception of freedom; we cannot think of proving its actual validity.

Now, in the first place, it should be remembered that 'freedom' and 'causality' are not absolutely opposed to each other, but are compatible with each other; that is to say, the former would postulate the latter, but of course the latter would not the former. For every free beginning of an action must demand that, in the world into which it intends to introduce an event a, all Things cohere firmly and according to law; so that from a only the intended result z can follow, and not any other at pleasure. Consequently 'freedom' is only to be accepted in the sense of an influence upon a world causally ordered.

Since however the free action ought to be subjected to an ethical judgment, it must be added that the decision with respect also to what is 'good' or 'bad,' is made in entire independence of the will. Therefore, freedom also is to be accepted only in the sense of a choice between what has value and what has not value, — permanently, and for its own sake.

The further objection, — namely that a freedom, in the sense intended by us, that is in the disreputable sense of a completely 'unconditioned' choice between a and non-a, is in respect of the process of its action incomprehensible, — is likely to be misunderstood: it does not raise a special obstacle such as positively to prohibit the conception of freedom, but simply and absolutely denies its validity. For, assuming that there is freedom, it is involved in its very conception, that the process of the decision it makes cannot be a 'comprehensible' one; because this would presuppose that the decision follows as the consequence of a succession of reciprocally conditioning circumstances, and therefore does not follow freely. If now offence is still taken at this incomprehensibility of freedom, it may be borne in mind, that the process of causal action would be no less obscure, and the fact of something effectuating something else, as regards its succession of events, just as incomprehensible.

If then it is still argued, that at all events such a capacity of choosing arbitrarily and blindly between a and non-a is irrational and unworthy of any respect, it is to be considered that we in fact neither commend nor venerate the 'freedom' that has not yet decided. It is only the 'will' which is no longer free, but has made its decision, that merits commendation or censure. 'Freedom' is simply the *conditio sine qua non* for the possibility of the subsequent valuation of the determinate act of willing.

For although we may concede that it is just the volition itself which we commend or censure, while we do not demand that this volition itself be repeated once more, still we after all tacitly presuppose in such a case, that just this 'volition' from the very outset has the significance of a decision sprung from 'freedom.' If this is denied us, and the will is defined as an emotion which originates mechanically within us, then we deny that ethical predicates are at all applicable to the will as a mere process of nature.

On the other hand it is objected, that the Good ought to be chosen for its own sake, but not in an entirely arbitrary manner: a blind freedom therefore would be just as little conducive to actions which may be judged ethically. In reply to this it is to be observed, that we can never speak of a 'blind' will; since all volition belongs to the same spiritual subject, which on the other hand is endowed likewise with the consciousness of the possible modes of its action and of their values. If such a subject in possession of this consciousness makes a choice, its choice at all events is not 'blind.' But there is no necessity for apprehending the presence in consciousness of the correct estimate of the possible modes of action as at the same time a determining influence which necessarily conditioned the direction of the will.

One difficulty however remains. The act of volition, although itself not causally conditioned, would still, if there is to be any corresponding result, be obliged to have a varying influence upon the existing states of the mind. And now the question comes, as to the means that determined the intensity with which the 'freely' originated will either overcomes the states of passion that struggle against it, or else yields to them. It would be a somewhat sophistical piece of information to affirm unqualifiedly that only the volition, but not the accomplishment of it is free; and indeed to carry this to such extent, that not only the possibility of the execution of an external action when willed would be doubtful, but that even the inner states of the mind also would form for the will a sort of external world, in which it could validate itself only in case the states of the same are moreover in harmony with its demands.

In a somewhat indefinite form this thought appears in the sphere of religion: we pray God to grant strength to the well-disposed but weak will; we therefore certainly ascribe volition to the human spirit, and only doubt about its needful power.

A decisive judgment upon this question it is hardly possible to find. To assume an entirely free 'volition' and to include in the conception of it its complete ineffectiveness seems almost absurd: on the contrary the other extreme opinion is a very bold one and hardly to be accepted; namely, that just as the will freely determines its own direction, so also is it able to determine its own intensity, and that it is always the willing spirit's own fault, if it has too little intensity of volition to overcome the involuntary psychical impulses to action.

§ 62. According to the entire foregoing discussion, acceptance or rejection of freedom will ultimately be a matter of decision, and not the result of a theoretical demonstration.

It is only on the assumption, that we do not hold the speculative difficulties which we encounter to be insuperable, and that we therefore believe in the freedom of spiritual beings, that there is any further interest in discussing the conception of a government of the world.

Government, in contradistinction to Preservation, could only consist in immediate influences of God upon the order of nature, such as were not included in the proper consequences of this order. And these influences could only be occasioned by the free actions which threaten to turn the progress of the world's course aside from a prescribed line.

Such divine influences are comprehended under the name of Miracles.

In order to estimate this conception, it must not be defined as an abolition of the order of nature in general, or of the general laws of nature. For then the conception would not at all correspond to what we mean by it. 'General' susspension of the 'laws of nature' would only occasion a chaos which is utterly beyond the power of representation.

The 'miracle' however is supposed to be a definite event, in which, in a single instance and with reference to definite things and for definite moments, the physical laws are invalidated which, contemporaneously or previously and subsequently, continued to be valid with respect to all other things.

This however means nothing but that the nature *a* of some one element experiences a change into α, by which it now no longer falls under the domain of the natural law g, but under that of another γ; and in consequence of this it no longer produces the ordinary effect, but another and extraordinary one. According to this definition, therefore, the miracle in general would involve no alteration whatever of the laws of nature, but only the change of one or more magnitudes to which those laws are applied.

Now it cannot be disputed, that such a change of the natures of single elements by the influence of a divine intervention is just as thinkable as it would be if accomplished by the intervention of another, and that a physical force. And particularly under the presupposition, that the Things of nature are not independent, but are products constantly supported by a divine power, does this general conception of the miracle contain, on the one hand, all that can be demanded in the religious interest, and, on the other, nothing that would be theoretically contradictory or impossible.

§ 63. There is no cause for overmuch rejoicing on account of this proof of the mere abstract conceivableness of the miracle. On the contrary it must be lamented, that we lack every decisive scientific regulative for determining the limits, within which we may have confidence in this possibility of thought, as valid in actuality. Only very indefinite thoughts upon this question admit of being presented.

That the order of nature for its own sake is in need of no corrections, is obvious. And the changes, which the free actions of spirits are able to produce in it, are so narrowly limited and may be so easily compensated for by the general economy of nature, that even for their sake 'miraculous' interventions are incredible.

Although, on the other hand, we feel a certain æsthetic inclination to behold great crises of history, in which a new phase of spiritual development has its beginning, made glorious by extraordinary changes of physical conditions also; still we must acknowledge that we can prove neither the necessity nor the real benefit which would result from satisfying our fancy by this summons of the miraculous.

It seems therefore, that it is not at all nature directly, but primarily the inner life of the world of spirits only, that forms the object, to which immediate interventions in the government of the world could have relation; and this in such manner that the interventions would not make use of the individual spirits merely as passive points of transition, but would supply their own activity with inducements and incentives, which the external course of nature cannot offer them. Moreover, by means of these inducements and incentives they would succeed, in accordance with the ordinary laws of the spiritual life, in introducing into the world new beginnings of spiritual movement that are in conformity with the plan of the world.

If in these events we include among others religious visions also, then we do not conceive them to be, as Rationalism does, merely subjective delusions to which nothing in external nature, and consequently nothing whatever corresponds. On the contrary, we think of them as products of a reciprocal action of God with individual spirits by means of which there is brought to pass in them an ideal appearance of a truly valid content; and this content would gain nothing whatever in dignity, value or reality, if it were realized, not merely as such appearance, but as physical or material actuality besides.

§ 64. Accordingly it is impossible speculatively to determine, how far within the limits of probability, faith in the applicability of the not essentially impossible conception of miracle ought to be extended.

The entire thought however, in which the inclination towards this faith has its source, is still further in harmony with the idea of a history for the world in which we come to participate with God in some common experience. And while this is something which is determined in accordance with his most general plan, it is still in its details by no means the mere result of original predestination. It is therefore not merely 'development' according to the law of reason and consequent, but actual history; and this history is without exception found only where general laws or a general plan are not executed with perfect constancy, but in alternate action with innumerable lawless obstacles or free counteractions.

This summing-up of actuality into a history which has beginning, middle and end, is very natural to all religions. And yet there are no doubt difficulties involved in such an idea in itself considered.

That is to say, it seems to us at first as if the proper determination of actuality consists in the historical actualization of a "world-aim" or in the struggle toward it. And with this understanding of the matter, it is altogether natural to regard the creation, the history of the world, and the judgment of the world, as three successive acts of such a concluded drama. But upon closer consideration after all this view is in contradiction to our needs.

If the world was created in time, so that reckoning from this (present) moment a retrogressive cognition should, after a finite number of steps, discover its beginning, then we are troubled by the emptiness of infinite time before this beginning; and we know of nothing with which to fill it out. For even the thought of a solitary preëxistence of God is an obscure one, supposing that the creation of the world is made to originate from an act of the will of God, which could have no need of this preparatory period either for its origination or for its execution.

Just so if the judgment of the world is the conclusion of history, it certainly cannot be understood to mean that the created actuality would now vanish again into nothingness. Rather is it only by this judgment of the world that there is established an order of things which fulfils the aim of the world, and which would then naturally be perpetuated *ad infinitum* as the actuality of that which ought to be; — and this without experiencing any further history of that development, which would now be superfluous.

Such considerations convince us that the idea

of these three successive periods of Beginning, Realization and Completion of an aim, — derived as it is from our human endeavors, — is not applicable to the totality of the world.

CHAPTER VIII.

OF THE CONCEPTION OF THE 'WORLD-AIM.'

§ 65. The conception of a 'world-aim,' which, according to the remarks we have just made, would not be realized all at once at the conclusion of a history, but progressively in the course of the world, we have simply introduced without any question as to its validity. Speculatively it is by no means to be demonstrated; it continues to be perfectly possible to think of the course of the world as an entirely purposeless, although more or less living development of an Absolute.

But religious feeling has an immediate evidence that the case is not so, and that all the phenomena of inspiration, of adoration, and of the feeling of obligation to an ideal, are not explicable as casual effects in the development of a purposeless Principle.

But if the conception of a supreme aim for the world is once acknowledged, then the other ideas, which form its necessary points of relation, comport with it; and especially the idea of a personal God, in whose consciousness and will alone this aim, previous to its full accomplishment, can have any actuality by means of which it becomes effective as guiding principle for the course of the world itself. To this subject however we are not going to return. The most urgent question is, wherein are we to place this 'supreme aim.'

§ 66. The answer to the foregoing question is to this extent self-evident, that naturally this aim cannot be placed in the realization of a fact, with respect to which the further question were possible ; why just this, and not other conceivable aims of like nature, is to fill this supremely exalted position in the world. The aim must obviously be that which has supreme value, and with respect to which the aforesaid question becomes senseless.

Now as to what this aim is, the common, unphilosophical religious view is not at all uncertain : nothing but the conception of blessedness seems to it to express this value, with respect to which it is absurd to raise the question, why this and why nothing else constitutes the supreme aim. It may be incidentally remarked, that the existence of a world of spirits is connected with the foregoing view as something conceivable. For only such a world could contain the subjects whose states this supreme aim may be conceived to be. On the other hand, this view by no means also furnishes at once an explanation of the existence of this determinate, *in*animate world.

§ 67. The above-mentioned view is combated in vain from the side of an ethical Rigorism, which, through its well-known undervaluation of all 'pleasure,' always in the practical domain, regards nothing but disinterested obedience to the universal commands of duty as ethical; and therefore in the religious domain also would not in any case be disposed to acknowledge ' supreme blessedness ' as the final purpose of the world, — perhaps not, with any readiness, even as a tolerable consequence of that purpose.

With respect to this point we briefly remark as follows: If obedience or disobedience to an ethical law were to occasion not a trace of pleasure or pain to any sensitive being in the world, — whether God, angels, or men, — it would be utterly incomprehensible, why it is just the obedience and not the disobedience to the law that must have an obligatory force; since after all the effects of the two modes of conduct consist only in the production of different states of fact, one of which would be as indifferent as the other.

In a word, it is impossible to understand what

is to constitute the 'value' of any action, if its results are not able to produce some 'Good' somewhere in the world, or to increase the sum of already existing 'Good.' But while we designate Things, States and Events as 'Good,' it is after all only in so far as they are means for obtaining the only real and substantial 'Good'; and this latter always exists only in the pleasure of some sensitive spirit, and would vanish with the world of spirits completely from the realm of actuality.

No Ethics can avoid having regard to a purpose that is final and in itself of absolute value. No matter to what extent many rigorous systems formulate their highest ethical laws apparently without any such regard, still, in addition to the assurances that they are the highest laws, the conclusion must always be supplied: What then would be the result, if these laws were not obeyed?

§ 68. The foregoing assertions do not degrade morals. It is not meant by them, that the direct endeavor after happiness -- and that, too, after one's own happiness — should be the ethically praiseworthy motive of our action. On this point our conscience gives us sufficient instruction; since it interprets this endeavor as in itself considered indifferent and merely natural, but on the contrary interprets as ethically laudable only the endeavor to secure the happiness of others. Thus (as might be further proved) the command of 'benevolence' is, among all ethical commands, really the fundamental one; and only upon the assumption of it do all the rest receive their obligatory value.

On the other hand, in seeking a coherent view of the world, we have a speculative interest in the fact that the ethical commands, which we are able in practice to obey without any further question as to their origin, are not wholly lacking in coherence with the arrangement of the world.

That such arrangement therefore be reckoned to the account of the final purpose of blessedness, is a speculative claim, which we set up in the interest, to a certain extent, of our reverence for the world, but not for the satisfaction of our own wishes for happiness. We are naturally unable to avoid including our own welfare also in this comprehensive final purpose.

The foregoing are perhaps the incentives which in religious thought have led to this doctrine of blessedness. From these incentives are distinguished, and not to their advantage, at least as regards the intention, the philosophical systems which only in a practical way set up claims upon our obedience to universal ethical laws, but speculatively give us no enlightenment with respect to the ultimate end, to which properly this ceaseless expenditure of ethical energy is to lead.

§ 69. Certainly, the laudation alluded to above holds good only of the intention and not of the performance of this religious opinion. It is wrecked rather in the attempt, actually to deduce the necessity of the *present* world from the supreme purpose of blessedness.

The first objection certainly might be disregarded; namely, why this purpose could be accomplished at all only as a result of a course of the world, and why it could not be accomplished as well from the very beginning. At the foundation of such a question there really lies the logical error of regarding the conception of 'blessedness' or of 'pleasure in general' in this universal sense of it, as something realizable. But the 'pleasure' that is without content can no more exist than a sensation of 'color in general,' which were neither green nor blue. Every 'pleasure' is rather an altogether determinate one, which is distinguished, as to its intensity and coloring, from others, and in both respects is determined by the nature of the content of which it is an enjoyment.

Hence it may be made evident, that we are utterly unable to form any real idea of a blessedness without content, although we can form the name of it; that it is capable of realization rather only upon the supposition that there are actual relations of some sort, which constitute the object of enjoyment in this pleasure; and, finally, that even these relations cannot be as they will, but together must form an orderly arrangement of the world.

But no progress is made in the foregoing way; the postulates which are set up with respect to such an arrangement of the world, are always after all general and abstract. That they had to be realized now by means of just *these* substances, forces, organisms, and kinds of occurrence, which we discover empirically in the world, is in nowise to be proved.

Wonder at the fact that so many other kinds of existence were still possible, which however do not exist, can be modified but imperfectly by the intimation that our range of experience is narrow, and that perhaps there are realized in the extra-earthly world all the possibilities which we miss upon the surface of the earth. For since we have reason to think that the most general physical laws, which are valid with us, are valid also for all distant parts of the world, therefore the organizations also which are there found can only be such as are in accordance with these laws. There always remains as conceivable, however, an infinite manifoldness that might exist, if those laws were only different. We are therefore brought round to the new question: Why are the laws of nature, which are not necessities of thought but empirical, precisely as they are and not otherwise? This question is unanswerable; and in our religious faith we must be content to think of the given world as in fact called to the realization of the supreme purpose, without being able to investigate any further the grounds of this calling.

§ 70. The existence of evil in the world — and that too primarily of mere physical evil — brings our general assumptions still further into inexplicable contradiction with our data of facts.

It is sufficient to indicate in a word, how utterly fruitless are those ways of speaking which seek to apologize for evil by recognizing it only "in particulars," but maintaining "the harmony of the world as a whole." One needs only to reverse these utterances: "On the whole the world makes a beautiful figure indeed, but in particulars it is wretched," — in order to understand that such expressions give evidence merely of the good intention of the apology, but specify no ground for such an apology.

Moreover the assertion of that "harmony on the whole" is in fact by no means whatever to be demonstrated. We merely know that the world does not perish on account of its imperfections, but that both it and they continue together.

§ 71. All efforts to attain to clearness upon the above-mentioned subject, can only try to apologize for the evil that does not admit of being done away with by denial.

The first onset for this purpose consists in the assumption that evil is necessary; in other words that God, although having in view only the Highest Good, has nevertheless been bound in his creation to laws which have not permitted the unconditioned Good, but only the choice of the best world among many, all of which were imperfect.

The limitation of the divine Omnipotence which is involved in this view, might be tolerated to a certain extent, if the aforesaid general laws were really understood to be simply the eternal truths, which, as we saw, are nothing extraneous to God, but are only the proper *modus agendi* of his own spiritual activity. But there is nothing whatever in the whole world by which to prove that these eternal truths were to blame for the evils that are in the world. So far as we are in any way empirically acquainted with the course of things, and are able, according to its analogy, to judge of non-realized possibilities, an absolutely faultless world would not be at all inconsistent with those 'eternal truths.' The ground of evil, so far as we know, lies rather in those special facts and arrangements, which are in actual existence, but instead of which there might as well be others that were also on friendly terms with the aforesaid truths and yet would not lead to these evils.

Since now we must attribute the establishment of these special actualities to the creative will of God, the attempt in this way to make the origin of evil independent of the divine will would not succeed; for his omnipotence would have still further to be so limited that even the actual elements of the world and their original combinations would be regarded as something taken for granted, in the midst of which God would have to find himself existing, and from which He then would have to endeavor to secure the best result still possible (Leibnitz).

This would be not only a degradation of our conception of God from a religious point of view, but it would also be speculatively fruitless. For in order that the measurable influence upon the world, which is still attributed to such a God, might be able to exist at all, a second superior God would have to be assumed, who, in the manner previously discussed (§§ 16 ff.), would comprehend both of these now mutually indifferent members in one reciprocal action, and would prevail upon them to act upon each other.

§ 72. After the foregoing explanation which is intended as metaphysical, there is one of a pedagogic sort, that regards evil as a means of Good, that is of education and improvement.

But in the first place this view merely contemplates men, who alone are capable of education. But in the animal world as well physical evils appear; and that not at all in a sporadic manner, but so systematized that the terrible torture and destruction of one class of creatures by the rest belongs directly to the so-called order of Nature. No pedagogic can make this comprehensible. We can much sooner comprehend how earlier times in despair over this very fact set a 'bad Principle' in a dualistic manner over against the Good.

But even leaving this out of the account,— any education makes use of evil simply because the minds which it intends to affect, are psychologically so defectively organized, that without this intrinsically objectionable means the end would no longer be realized. If it were applied to the entire world, it would lead back to the previous thought: God did not have it in his power to make the world so perfect that it would attain its end without corrections by means of evil.

§ 73. A view which has been elaborated rather in a religious and mystical way, regards the morally Bad as prior and physical evil as a consequence of its becoming actual.

Now the circumstance that the truly Good was not to be actualized without the possibility of the Bad, and therefore that the freedom of the world of spirits was to be conceded, we can consider as a necessity which need not be foreign even to God's own nature. But after all we do not understand, why the bad disposition which entered the world in consequence of such freedom needed to have any physical result at all; and why the danger which it threatened to the undisturbed continuance of the world, was not averted by one of those self-compensations, by means of which so frequently elsewhere in nature the beginning of a disturbed equipoise cancels itself again.

The necessary existence of freedom would therefore by no means show that the innocent must suffer by its misuse. But in addition to this also the view does not cover the whole question.

For the further assumption that nature was originally without evil and that sin first brought it into the world, not only lacks all empirical foundation, but is even in itself considered untenable. We cannot, just because individual spirits, or even very many of them, erred, regard 'sin' as a unit-principle or a power which would have a legitimate influence upon the course of nature in general; still less is it to be understood, why nature did not endeavor to overcome singly the disturbances which the sin that is foreign to it had introduced, instead of admitting physical evils, as a kind of solidaric totality, into the very plan of its operations.

The incomprehensibleness of the foregoing views is not lessened by their being proclaimed with still greater emphasis; thus, for example, by speaking of a "voluntary fall of the entire creation" which now extends "the curse of its imperfection to all creatures that still spring from it." In whatever way the picture may be painted, to attribute this act of a 'fall' to the collective conception of a creation means after all nothing whatever. It is intelligible only as regards each particular, individual, free and conscious being. But if we refer it to such a being, then it is a perfect monstrosity, at variance with the simplest sense of justice, to assume that the consequences of this act pass over, as an inheritance which it is impossible to shake off, to all later generations, although they are according to their very conception destined to like 'freedom.'

In very different forms have Mythology, Mysticism and Dogmatics represented such a primæval history of the world. But none of these attempts has been able to eliminate the aforesaid manifest incongruities.

§ 74. The above-mentioned incapacity of our speculative cognition for the solution of this enigma of evil had to be very plainly expressed. For there ought not to remain any seeming as if there were, in expressions which cannot be understood and which only commend themselves to the imagination through intuitive images, any real speculative proof for the correctness of the religious feeling upon which rests our faith in a good and holy God, and in the destination of the world to the attainment of a blessed end.

He who does not share this religious conviction, may, on account of these last considerations of ours, very easily from a speculative point of view reach that Pessimism, which is just now the order of the day, and for which there will be on speculative grounds no refutation. But this Pessimism, which reverts to the thought of an original energy without will, that produces the Good and the Bad alike without design, is not a profound view but is just that cheap and superficial kind of view, by which all enigmas are conveniently disposed of — by simply sacrificing all that is most essential and supreme to the unprejudiced mind.

In contrast with this Pessimism, the more difficult problem is the firm confidence that, in spite of all that is incomprehensible to us, the striving after a supreme end is at all events extant in the world. For this confidence takes upon itself the great and ever unavoidable task of always making renewed attempts to fill the gap which lies between this content of our faith and our actual experiences.

If we call every attempt of this sort in thought or action 'Religion,' then 'religion' is never exactly a demonstrable theorem, but the conviction of its truth is a *deed* that is to be accredited to character.

CHAPTER IX.

RELIGION AND MORALITY.

§ 75. If there is no speculative argument for religious conviction, still there must be a motive for holding fast this conviction. And in fact an appeal has constantly been made to an 'immediate inner experience,' which attests the truth of the content of religion, as directly and independently of the intervention of logic as perception by the senses attests the reality of external objects. It has already been said in the Introduction however, that there by no means exists an harmonious inner experience as regards that divine order of the world which is not perceivable by the senses; but rather that (compare also § 59) the only element common to men, to which an appeal may be made for the confirmation of religion, consists in those 'utterances of the conscience' that primarily only say what *ought* to be, and yet after all permit an indirect inference from this as to what *is*.

§ 76. There are different ways of apprehending this real function of the 'conscience' also.

It must be acknowledged that the conscience is not, prior to all experience, a coherent revelation of the commands to which our future conduct ought to conform; the rather is it like our capacity of cognition. The supreme principles to which this capacity reduces its judgment of Things, are also no original ready-made possession of our consciousness. Particular perceptions rather induce us, in the first place, as a sort of immediate reaction, to effect their combination so as to give them a definite significance. It is only subsequent reflection upon many such particular cases, that shows us in accordance with what 'principles' our conduct, which was previously only instinctive, has proceeded. And now for the first time are they *conscious principles*, to which we conform in our subsequent cognition.

Just so 'conscience' is first induced, by considering cases that are quite definite, to pass particular judgments of approval or disapproval upon actions which are brought before it. It is only by reflective comparison of these particular judgments, that there is formed from them those general ethical precepts, which it is then customary to designate as the 'immediate voice of conscience.'

§ 77. This necessary concession with respect to the psychological development of our conscience, is now made use of to support in the first place a view, which annuls the obligatory value and the proper majesty of ethical commands.

It is the view, namely, that the sensibility which induces the spirit to approve or disapprove of some definite act itself rests in turn merely upon the immediate well-being or ill-being, which the spirit experiences from it. When however this sensibility proceeds to the formation of general propositions, it comprises only those maxims, constant obedience to which experience has taught secures on the average the highest degree and steadiest permanence of that well-being which is at all attainable. All ethical commands accordingly appear merely as maxims of that Egoism which seeks its own self-preservation; they appear however as *general* laws simply for the reason that the limitation of our cognition of the past, present and future, does not in every case permit that mode of action which is specially suited to these different periods, for the attainment of the highest possible good.

To this entire mode of apprehending the subject we must now concede this one point,— namely, that the mere experience of human intercourse certainly may furnish us with the concrete and determinate particular content of those precepts, in conforming to which ethical behavior consists; and that, on the other hand, all attempts in a reverse direction to deduce those specialized precepts from the general conceptions of the Good, the Ethical, the Holy, or the Just, are in vain. Such general conceptions express nothing whatever but the peculiar character of the impression, which definite kinds of conduct will make upon our feelings, as soon as we shall become acquainted with them: on the other hand, they do not acquaint us with just those forms of the conduct itself, to which this impression will apply.

§ 78. A disposition which insists upon endeavoring to find in ethical precepts nothing but prudential maxims acquired by experience, and to find back of all actions nothing but egoistic motives, can in no way be gainsaid by mere speculation. So much only is clear, namely, that such an interpretation of moral commands is *arbitrary*. For in that case also, supposing us to assume that a worth and sacredness of their own belongs to these commands, everything would still be exactly the same. That is to say, these commands would in fact be the maxims, conforming to which produces the greatest amount of happiness. The *content* moreover of that which they command would always be learned first by experience, as was previously mentioned. And for just this reason it would always be possible to represent them as though they were nothing more than such lessons of experience with respect to what is expedient.

But on the other hand, he who prefers this interpretation overlooks the fact, that we all of us none the less set over against the conduct which simply conforms to these maxims of prudence, another of an altogether different sort, as being the only one of value; and this latter conduct conforms to these same maxims, although with different sentiments; and indeed with such sentiments as either have disinterested regard to the establishment of the Good, in precisely the same way, for instance, in which we reverence beauty as having objective value without advantage to ourselves — or else with such sentiments as find happiness, so far as they make the production of it an object of pursuit, only in benevolence towards others and not in selfishness.

This also may be denied; but in denying it there is involved the denial of an inner experience, upon the acknowledgment of which every further upward flight of religion depends. Conversely, therefore, it will not be possible to gainsay those who are conscious of this inner experience.

§ 79. But even the recognition of the peculiar worth and sacredness of ethical commands does not lead at once to a *religious* view of the world; on the contrary this recognition, in ancient as well as modern times, has been put in express opposition to religious thoughts, which seemed like a needless and false supplement to it. It is not to be denied, that *practically* even this Stoicism, or the Rationalism which disdains any connection with religion, may, by mere subordination to the general demands of morality and of the course of the world, furnish the basis for a conduct of life well deserving of recognition. But there are involved in this conception (compare § 68) peculiar speculative contradictions.

It is maintained in the first place, that all thoughts about an origin at some time or other, or about an ultimate aim of moral laws, are to be avoided, because they could only serve to corrupt the conception of the peculiar sacredness and unconditioned obligation of these laws, which demand rather an altogether immediate recognition as being absolutely obligatory. Worthy of respect as is the sentiment which is thus expressed, yet the speculative thought, by which it would like to sustain itself, is utterly unserviceable. Laws that are completely unconditioned may be conceived of, so far forth as they in fact govern all actuality, like the laws of nature, and are consequently expressions of a '*must*' which knows *no* exceptions. On the contrary the thought of an 'unconditioned Ought,' that is, of a law to which actuality in no wise of itself corresponds, is incomprehensible.

There must be a difference between the reality of that which *ought* to be and of that which ought *not* to be; and this difference cannot consist in the mere repetition of these two antithetical predicates. Rather must the very consideration, that the one ought to be and the other ought not to be, have a practical validity. In other words and more simply: An unconditioned 'Ought' is unthinkable; and only a *conditioned* Ought is possible, which attaches advantages and disadvantages to the observance or non-observance of what is prescribed. These very consequences, however, may still consist ultimately only in pleasure or pain. And in this alone also consists the 'absolute value,' as it is called, which the ideals of conduct designated by moral laws possess. A value, which is valued by *no one*, and therefore causes *no one* pleasure or pain, is, according to our previous explanation (§ 67), an essentially self-contradictory thought.

Now the advantage, which must be inseparably connected with the claim to validity for the moral laws, could be sought primarily in that immobility of feeling, that *ataraxy*, which Stoicism regards as the ideal of life for the wise man. But if this is commendable so far as it does not permit disturbance by the passions, still there is little that is commendable in its consequence, which would also exclude living enthusiasm for the Good and Beautiful, and would virtually degrade the feeling spirit to the form in which an impersonal substance exists. The moral laws, however, so far as this *ataraxy* would be attained by observing them, would in fact still be mere maxims of utility, which would be designed for the attainment of a completely egoistic well-being.

It is manifestly, however, not this tranquillity of mind alone that has been in view as the ultimate goal and good, but the self-esteem which is secured by observance of the moral laws. Now this may without doubt be very well meant, but to say the least it is not compatible with the refusal of all further religious views. If we regard the individual personality as only a product of nature, which transiently appears and then vanishes, it is not possible to understand just why we attach any value to the fact that what we revere as good and holy must have its realization in just such an 'Ego' as this. Self-esteem also would therefore be immediately intelligible as an ultimate goal only in case it were brought under the conception of that which ministers to our egoistic well-being, in the same way as does every sensuous satisfaction. It would be possible for it to have a different significance only in case our view of our own personality, and of its position in the totality of the world be changed.

§ 80. The foregoing reflections, which confessedly have not the value of demonstrations in the proper sense, but are merely intended to make us sensible of the connection by which the particular thoughts here mentioned, first get their complete satisfaction, lead us now to three propositions which we may regard as the characteristic convictions of every religious apprehension, in contradistinction to a merely intellectual view of the world, — namely:

(1) Ethical laws we designate as the will of God;

(2) Individual finite spirits we designate not as products of nature, but as children of God;

(3) Actuality we designate not as a mere course of the world, but as a kingdom of God. These three propositions are to be elucidated and their consequences investigated.

§ 81. The first of the above-mentioned propositions has raised objections, which ultimately lead to the well-known scholastic alternative: 'Is the Good good, because God wills it? or does He will it, because it is good?' This point is to be decided according to the analogy of the similar question as to the validity of eternal truths.

If one would answer the first member of the alternative in the affirmative, the question would be asked: What then is comprehended under the thought of that God, who appears here as the subject of this will? He would be nothing but an infinite Power, as yet wholly devoid of content; and the affirmation, that He has willed the Good (if it meant a determination of will issued in time, quite as much as if it declared this will, to be one without beginning and eternal) would really be precisely identical with the other assertion, — namely, the Good is assumed to be once for all in existence, and a 'positing' or 'affirming,' wholly without origin, is the basis of this assumption. It is moreover obvious, that every such deed of mere power, while it may impart *necessity*, cannot impart *worth* to the command.

But then, on the other hand, it is just as fruitless to assert that God wills the Good because it is 'intrinsically good.' For, to say nothing about the ambiguity of this latter expression, an acknowledgment of the Good, which is not a merely enforced decree in subordination to a statute, would after all be possible only in case the content to be acknowledged already possesses for the nature of the acknowledging spirit the truth and the value which is to be awarded to it.

We are convinced therefore, that the abovementioned alternative separates again two thoughts, which must be thought together in absolute inseparableness as the expression of a single fact; and that we always run against absurdities, whenever we make one of these alternatives the condition for the other.

We therefore come to the following decision: God is nothing else than that Will, whose content and modes of procedure are comprehended in our reflection as the 'intrinsically Good'; and which may by abstraction be separated from that living form of existence which it nowhere else possesses but precisely in the real God. In truth, however, such will of God no more follows from his nature as secondary to it, or precedes it as primary to it, than in motion — say direction can be antecedent or subsequent to velocity.

It is therefore an entire mistake to object that

the peculiar majesty of moral laws suffers detriment if they are regarded as the will of God. For we take this view of the matter, not precisely with the design of laying, by the specification of their origin, a basis for that worth of those commands which we directly recognize; but we do it in order to add to this worth — which, although it stands on its own foundation, we were nevertheless obliged to regard speculatively as an incomplete thought, — this supplement, by which, as we remarked, its worth is not enhanced but becomes intelligible and compatible with the totality of our view of the world.

§ 82. As regards the second proposition (§ 80), the somewhat sentimental way in which it is expressed need not deceive us with respect to the weightiness of the thought. It has a twofold meaning. That is to say, on the one hand there is involved in it the recognition of the finiteness of the personal spirit and of its subjection to the power and wisdom of God. And herein is found the reason for that opposition which the Christian Religion especially has expressed against the pride of speculative systems of morality, that seek to attain as their ideal the self-satisfaction, self-esteem, and self-righteousness of the 'wise man.'

The other part of this twofold meaning is the no less lively opposition to that depreciation of personality, which sees in it merely a transient product of the course of nature. The assertion is therefore expressed in this connection, that there exists between man and God a relation of piety; that this relation is always a vital one; and that by means of it — but also *only* by means of it — the finite spirit ceases to be such absolutely dependent product of the course of nature.

The hope of being loved by God, however, takes the place of mere self-satisfaction as the Highest Good. Such approval by the Supreme Spirit supplants the proud claim of having one's satisfaction in one's own self-esteem.

§ 83. With relation to the third proposition (§ 80), we have already been obliged to confess that we do not know the content and plan of the divine government of the world: and the consequence of this with respect to religion is, that the entire consideration of external reality is withdrawn from its domain, and is regarded as an object for science, which has to ascertain its consistence by methods entirely free from prejudice, and therefore not at all influenced even by religious considerations.

This attitude, too, is distinctive of Christianity.

The religions of heathenism possess a mythology, which seeks to explain and interpret, in a very circumstantial manner, the facts of reality. Christianity has no mythology and rests all its reflections entirely upon considerations of the spiritual world, of which we have an inner experience.

CHAPTER X.

DOGMAS AND CONFESSIONS.

§ **84.** Nothing more than the content of the three propositions already cited is in fact revealed, even by the Christian Revelation. To be penetrated by their influence, and to be voluntarily subject to the divine will, as they require, constitutes a living, consolatory religious state, — or religion as a condition of mind.

It is, nevertheless, quite impossible to avert attempts to transform this religious content, which was originally apprehended only in living presentiment, into a series of formulated and communicable propositions.

To such attempts we are impelled on the one side by our own life-experience, which desires to answer the doubts that have arisen, not always by a mere appeal to the same frame of mind, but also by convictions that enter upon the special content of the doubts raised. Under the name of religious Mysticism may be summed up the whole of these attempts at theory which are based exclusively upon one's own inner religious experience, and which also primarily claim no other validity than that which exists for the personal subject who finds out of the depth of his own mind the desired answers to those doubts.

§ 85. Over against this first impulse stands a second. It is essentially self-contradictory for one to stand alone with his religious conviction, since it is just this condition which unites man to the entire universe. Religion is not merely union of the individual with God, but in and by this union it is at the same time union with all other men.

In this impulse lies the one respectable root of religious Fanaticism. What we acknowledge as the Supreme, would not be such *Supreme*, unless it were acknowledged by all. Hence now there follows, not the warrant to be sure to force one's subjective views upon others, but rather that need of a religious community — now so frequently mistaken — within which each one finds again, not indeed the complete content of his own individual mysticism, but at least the outlines of the conviction to which he is able to subordinate or to attach his own.

Such therefore is the necessity of generally accepted Dogmas and Symbols.

§ 86. Without doubt the historic development of such thoughts will embrace the content of religion more completely than the life-experience of an individual; although this latter pervades with greater intensity that which has once become object of such personal experience.

Generally accepted objective dogmas will therefore have the twofold design, — on the one hand, to hold fast those solutions of doubt which have been gained in the course of time; but, on the other hand, to designate certain outlines of thought beyond which our subjective fancies are not to go without exposing themselves to error.

According to our previous considerations, no one of these dogmas would be, properly speaking, a speculatively or scientifically conclusive answer to a proposed question; they would all be mere symbols rather, which acknowledge the existence of an enigma and which by means of an insufficient figurative designation only fix the limits of that range of thoughts, beyond which the fulfilment of such postulates must not be sought.

It would therefore be reckoned a mistake for us to demand of the one who purposes to belong to a religious community, an obligation binding him to the literal purport of such dogmas. It is just according to their literal purport that they cannot be objects of a confession or non-confession at all. In order that this question of confession may be raised, the dogmas need at all times an interpretation of their real meaning, — a meaning which they always indicate but imperfectly, by figures or symbols. Such interpretation however is not given objectively, but each individual is in fact to find it by the activity of his own mind.

It appears therefore that the only question to be put to the one who proposes to belong to a religious community is, whether he in his own heart experiences and confesses a religious truth, which admits of being comprehended as the import of this objectively formulated dogma, and which it is worth while to have acknowledged in this particular form as a bond of union for the religious conviction of a collective body.

§ 87. It may be objected, that there is involved in this a sort of dissimulation. But above all things we do *not* maintain that religion and its dogmas are obligatory 'only for the uncultivated.' The truth of religion rather is absolutely valid for all alike; on the contrary, the speculative expressions which have been discovered for it, are altogether inadequate. And for just this reason it is permitted to agree upon a formula, to which each one gives that theoretical construction by which he believes its essential meaning is best comprehended.

In other departments of life also we are not able to discard methods of apprehending the world, which within the sphere of philosophy we nevertheless recognize as inadequate. The existence of a space-world outside of us, the atoms, and the forces of matter, — all these are ideas, without the use of which not only the common understanding, but even philosophy, which denies their correctness, would not be at all able to find its way in its observation and treatment of the external world. In all these cases it is not so much that we get at the truth, as that we get at such an intuitive '*seeming*' as is able to make intelligible to us the essentially inexpressible, but true relations of the Actual.

Just so in the case of religion it is not required that there be found a speculatively unobjectionable expression for that which 'is essentially Transcendent, but that we have figurative expressions to which the mind may attach the same feelings that are appropriate to the proper content of religion.

Now it is of course to be conceded that we could speak as simply as we do, only in case these formulated dogmas were first to be established. They are however already in existence, and historically considered they are surely not in all cases so perfected, that they admit of no misunderstanding as to their true sense. But still this affords no reason for a wilful separation from those circles which acknowledge the dogmas; it only involves a summons not to make of them subjects for theoretic instruction, as well as a problem of pastoral wisdom in combating the evils of a false interpretation.

§ 88. The attempts at theory may be reduced to three divisions, the first of which only, Theology in the narrower sense, is sufficiently accessible to philosophy.

We have endeavored in the preceding discussion to show, what more precise determinations of the Divine Being philosophy admits, what it excludes, and finally what it demands, without being able to present them in the form of adequate conceptions. As the total result of our discussion we repeat, that faith in a personal God contradicts none of those metaphysical convictions which we are compelled to maintain; that, on the contrary, those assertions are entirely without foundation which, with decided incredulity as regards all that is religious and with frivolous credulousness as regards the theories fashionable in physical science, conceive of an origin for spiritual life from the forces of mere matter; and, finally, that the charge of anthropomorphism is entirely unjust, for the distinctions between the infinite and the finite spirit are by no means overlooked. But it is certainly foolish to prefer to assign the Supreme Principle of the world to an unconscious blind substratum, the conception of which is for us, strictly speaking, something completely dark and inscrutable.

§ 89. Further speculations — as for example concerning the Trinity — would be, as regards the religious life, matters of complete indifference, but for the fact that they have been brought into connection with the position toward God, which the human race has come to occupy by means of the establishment or revelation of religion. The consideration in general of this position forms a second grand object of religious theories.

According to the conviction maintained in this discussion as to the constant activity of God in the world and upon individual spirits; and considering our acknowledged ignorance of the precise plan which the divine government follows; there is nothing whatever that stands in opposition to the further conviction that God, at particular moments and in particular persons, may have stood nearer to humanity, or may have revealed himself at such moments and in such persons in a more eminent way than at other moments and in other persons.

If therefore reverence for the founder of our religion designates him as 'Son of God,' no serious objection to the essential thought which is expressed by this term is, in view of the preceding paragraph, tenable; it is even without doubt legitimate to regard the relation in which he stood to God, as absolutely unique not only as to degree but also as to its essential quality.

But no one can discover an *adequate* expression for that which would exactly correspond to the connotation of such a term (diesen Intentionen). Since then Christ after all cannot be 'God's Son' in the literal sense, but the true meaning of this figurative expression admits of no authentic interpretation whatever, this entire proposition is not at all adapted for the formation of a speculative dogma; and he who assents to it in fact expresses merely his conviction of the unique value which Christ has for him, and which Christ's relation to God has for humanity, without however being able precisely to define either of them.

§ 90. He who in an unprejudiced way allows the teaching of Christ and the history of Christ's life to influence his mind, without analyzing this impression, may be convinced that an infinitely valuable and unique act has occurred here on earth for the salvation of humanity. But the attempts to settle speculatively the content and value of this fact, do not as a whole lead to the end designed.

It is impossible to speak of God's honor as receiving '*satisfaction*' through the sacrificial death of a single person, for the injury done it by the sin of man. For such a view, aside from its somewhat crude conception of God, is based upon the altogether impossible conception of a solidaric unity of the human race and of the possibility of a transfer of its guilt and obligation to a single representative.

The more humane ideas of a 'Reconciliation' or a 'Redemption' — at least the latter of them — leave it undetermined from whom it is, precisely, that humanity beholds itself delivered by this ransom. It could not well be God, but must rather be the order of natural law, which has connected sin with our finiteness and condemnation with our sin.

Now we know that we are redeemed neither

from physical evils nor from the possibility of sin. The only thing left therefore as the practically effective result of redemption is the content of a faith revealed and proffered to us, which redeems us from the distress and wretchedness of Creation, in so far as it teaches us to regard all evil as only a divine trial; teaches us, however, to regard the whole of the earthly life, not to be sure as insignificant, nor yet as an irrevocable finality, but as a state of preparation, for the errors of which there is in the divine grace a redemption which we are not in the least able speculatively to define.

All further speculations which attach themselves to this subject — as, for example, about the origin of sin and about its consequences — are perfectly useless as regards the religious life.

§ 91. Even the third division of such speculations, which we may sum up as Eschatology, does not admit of being cultivated speculatively. The earthly future of the human race as well as the nature of our immortality and of the retribution which the final judgment will bring, are entirely beyond the reach of any concrete portrayal. And in this connection the Humanism of modern times has in fact become entirely disused to such concrete representations, and has become satisfied, as it must be, with maintaining the general faith in continued existence and in a constant process of perfection, as well as in a retribution; and in just this way it has shown that for a truly religious life there is really no necessity whatever for that vast sum of knowledges which dogmatics, with much liability to misunderstanding, assumes as necessary to such a life.

§ 92. Mention was previously made of the value attaching to the necessity that one shall not stand alone in his religious convictions. The value of this is the more enhanced on account of the fact that the content of these very convictions themselves consists in faith in an uninterrupted union of men with each other and with God, into which it is possible for every one to enter by his own free choice.

If we call this communion the invisible Church, then the visible Church, on the other hand, is certainly nothing more than a human institution of the company of believers: partly for fellowship in the worship of God, partly for the regulation of its earthly affairs in agreement with the demands of its faith. But every pretension which such visible Church might advance, not merely to teach the way to eternal salvation and to guide to it, but to open and to shut this way by virtue of its own power, is quite unfounded. As for the rest, the Church, like every other institution, must not fall into a condition of opposition to the regulations of the State; although we cannot regard it as a happy expression to say that the Church must be *subjected* to these regulations in anything else but external matters of an altogether indifferent character. On the contrary, it is the evil of the present time — and of course has its historic conditions — that the State as such is compelled to exist without any religious foundation and that it believes it has no need of any.

But the complete unity of the State in religious matters also, would of course presuppose that two hostile parties should return to modesty; — namely, that theological learning on the one side, and irreligious natural science on the other, should not assert that they have exact knowledge about so very much which they neither do know nor can know; it would therefore presuppose that, in the recognition of divine mysteries which are left to the interpretation of each individual believing mind, and of general ethical precepts concerning the meaning of which moreover there exists no controversy, the religious life may unfold itself in accordance with the motto: *In necessariis unitas, in dubiis libertas, in omnibus caritas.*

INDEX.

INDEX.

A.

Absolute, the One Being, 32 f.; relation of Things to, 33 f.; Determinations of, 35 f.; Spinoza's view of, 38; as personal Spirit, 43 f., 55 f., 68; and therefore conscious, 66 f.; none besides God, 83 f.; course of the world related to, 114 f.
Action, between elements, 25 f.; of Things on each other, 30 f.
Argument, the Ontological, 8 f.; the Cosmological, 10 f.; the Teleological.
Attributes, of God, 45 f.

B.

Being, God as the Most Perfect, 9 f.; as the necessary, 10 f.; and unconditioned, 13 f., 55 f.; intelligent, 21; the Absolute, 32 f.; Unity of, 52 f.
Blessedness, as the supreme end, 118 f.

C.

Christ, as Son of God, 150 f.; relation to humanity, 150.
Church, visible and invisible, 153; relation of, to State, 153.
Conscience, function of, 129 f.; development of, 131 f.
Consciousness, belongs to Personality, 56 f.; conception of, 56; origin of, 57 f.; involves self-identical Ego, 59 f., 62; feeling necessary to, 60 f.
Contingent, events, as, 10 f.
Creation, conception of, 71 f.; Divine will in, 73 f.; not necessarily *deed*, 74 f., 79 f.; "out of Nothing," 79; no process of, 79 f.

D.

Design, conscious in Nature, 17 f.
Development, not creation, 71 f., 79.
Dogmas, necessity of, 143 f.; subscription to, 145; limits of, 147.
Dualism, in philosophy, 39; as to origin of evil, 124.

E.

Ego, unites elements, 30; idea of, 59 f., 63, 64; correlative to non-ego, 62 f.
End, conformity to an, 16 f., 18 f.; in the world's history, 111 f., 114; the supreme, 115 f., 118.
Eschatology, not a matter for speculation, 152.
Ethics, relation of, to the idea of value, 117; and of expediency, 132 f.
Evil, apologies for, 121 f.; origin of, 124, 126.

F.

Faith, as organ of Religion, 1 f.
Fall, conception of a, 126 f.
Fanaticism, origin of, 144.
Feeling, groups of the religious, 5 f.; necessary to self-consciousness, 60 f.
Fichte, on "world-stuff," 97.
Force, conception of, in Nature, 17 f., 20 f.; blind and unconscious, 40.
Freedom, a condition of Government, 99; not speculatively defensible, 100 f., 102, 106; objections to, 103.

G.

God, proof of his existence, 8 f.; ontological argument for, 8 f.; cosmological argument for, 10 f.; as unconditioned, 13 f.; teleological argument for, 15 f., 22 f., 24 f.; as Supreme Intelligence, 21; Unity of, 45 f.; Unchangeableness of, 46 f., 52 f.; Omnipresence of, 47 f.; Omnipotence of, 49 f., 86 f., 88; Eternity of, 51 f.; Personality of, 55 f., 68 f.; as Creator, 70, 79; productive will of, 73 f., 79 f., 139; no Principle antecedent to, 82, 90; relation of truth to, 84 f., 91 f.; government of, 95 f.
Good, idea of the highest, 122, 133, 141; as compatible with Evil, 124; relation to the Divine Will, 138 f.
Government, the Divine, 95 f.; conditions of, 98 f., 106; distinguished from Preservation, 107; by intervention, 109 f.

I.

Intelligence, in Nature, 21; inhering in Things, 24 f.

L.

Law, not *above* Things, 83; nor antecedent to God, 83 f., 88 f.
Leibnitz, best possible world of, 123.

M.

Materialism, its account of self-consciousness, 57.
Matter, contrasted with Spirit, 35 f., 37, 38.
Metaphysic, Postulates derived from, 30 f., 52.
Miracle, the conception of, 107 f.; abstract conceivableness of, 108 f.; extent not speculatively determined, 110 f.
Mysticism, origin of, 143.

N.

Nature, elements and forces of, 18 f.; blind course of, 21 f., 47.
Necessary, conception of the, 10, 12 f.

O.

Omnipotence, meaning of the Divine, 49, 86 f., 88; never in the abstract, 87 f.; *modus agendi* of, 122.
Ought, idea of the, 135 f.

P.

Pantheism, 38.
Personality, conception of, 55 f.; of the Absolute, 55, 68; a self-conscious ego, 59 f., 62 f., 64; perfect only when infinite 68 f.
Pessimism, 128.
Philosophy, legitimate place of, 1 f.
Power, conception of, 87 f.
Preservation, of the World, 81 f., 92 f.; as new creation, 92 f.
Principle, the absolute, 35; and the supreme, 149.
Providence, in organism, 22 f.

R.

Reason, organ of Religion, 1 f.; necessarily self-conscious, 39 f.
Redemption, idea of, 151 f.
Religion, as related to Reason, 1 f., 6; and scientific cognition, 4 f.; involves experience, 5; feelings of, 5 f.; relation to morals, 129 f.; first principles of, 137; the Christian, 140; the communion of, 145.
Rigorism, an ethical, 116 f.

S.

Schelling, 38.
Science, nature of its cognitions, 4.
Sensations, origin of, 36.
Sin, origin of, in a Fall, 126 f.
Spinoza, 38.
Spirit, contrasted with Matter, 35 f., 38; always self-conscious, 39, 56 f.; and personal, 41 f.; the Infinite, 66; finite spirits, 67 f., 96.
Spiritualism, the philosophical, 39.
Stoicism, its wise man, 136.

T.

Theology, relation to philosophy, 148.
Things, properties of, 16 f.; as intelligent, 24 f.; homogeneous and connected, 29 f., 31; influence of, on each other, 30 f.; as modifications of the Absolute, 32 f., 34, 67; spiritual susceptibility of, 37; cannot have unity, 53; as subject to law, 83.
Time, not self-subsisting form, 51 f.
Trinity, doctrine of, 149.
Truth, as related to God, 84 f., 91 f.

U.

Unconditioned, conception of the, 13 f.
Universe, origin of, 17 f., 28; elements of, 27 f., 28 f.

W.

Will, the Divine in creation, 73 f.; the human, 75, 104; *modus agendi* unknown, 77; the free, 104 f.
World, relation of, to God, 70, 81, 94, 95.

THE BEST HISTORIES.

MYERS'S Eastern Nations and Greece. — Introduction price, $1.00. With full maps, illustrations, and chronological summaries.

"Far more interesting and useful than any other epitome of the kind which I have yet seen." — Professor BECKWITH, *Trinity College.*

ALLEN'S Short History of the Roman People. — Introduction price, $1.00. With full maps, illustrations, and chronological synopsis.

"An admirable piece of work." — Professor BOURNE, *Adelbert College.*

MYERS AND ALLEN'S Ancient History for Schools and Colleges. — Introduction price, $1.50. This consists of Myers's Eastern Nations and Greece and Allen's Rome bound together.

MYERS'S History of Rome. — Introduction price, $1.00. With full maps, illustrations, tables, and chronological summaries.

"Though condensed, the style is attractive and will interest students." — Professor SPROULL, *University of Cincinnati.*

MYERS'S Ancient History. — Introduction price, $1.50. This consists of Myers's Eastern Nations and Greece and History of Rome bound together.

MYERS'S Mediæval and Modern History. — Introduction price, $1.50. With a full series of colored maps.

"Sure to be liked by teachers and pupils and by the general reader." — Professor SNOW, *Washington University.*

MYERS'S General History. — Introduction price, $1.50. With full maps, illustrations, tables, and summaries.

"The best text-book in universal history for beginners that we are acquainted with." — Professor STEARNS, *University of Wisconsin.*

MONTGOMERY'S Leading Facts of English History. — Introduction price, $1.12. With full maps and tables.

"I have never seen anything at all equal to it for the niche it was intended to fill." — Professor PERRY, *Princeton College.*

MONTGOMERY'S Leading Facts of French History. — Introduction price, $1.12. With full maps and tables.

"It is a marked advance on any available work of its scope." — *The Nation.*

MONTGOMERY'S Leading Facts of American History. — Introduction price, $1.00. With full maps, illustrations, summaries of dates, topical analyses, tables, etc.

"The best school history that has yet appeared." — Principal RUPERT, *Boys' High School, Pottstown, Pa.*

EMERTON'S Introduction to the Study of the Middle Ages. — Introduction price, $1.12. With colored maps, original and adapted.

"An admirable guide to both teachers and pupils in the tangled period of which it treats." — Professor FISHER, *Yale College.*

And many other valuable historical works.

GINN & COMPANY, Publishers, Boston, New York, Chicago, and London.

MODERN LANGUAGE TEXT-BOOKS.

	INTROD. PRICE
Becker and Mora: Spanish Idioms	$1.80
Collar-Eysenbach: German Lessons	1.20
Shorter Eysenbach	1.00
Cook: Table of German Prefixes and Suffixes	.05
Doriot: Illustrated Beginners' Book in French	.80
Beginners' Book. Part II.	.50
Illustrated Beginners' Book in German	.80
Dufour: French Grammar	.60
French Reader	.80
Grandgent: German and English Sounds	.50
Hempl: German Grammar	.00
German Orthography and Phonology	.00
Knapp: Modern French Readings	.80
Modern Spanish Readings	1.50
Modern Spanish Grammar	1.50
Lemly: New System of Spanish Written Accentuation	.10
Smith: Gramática Práctica de la Lengua Castellana	.60
Spiers: French-English Dictionary	4.50
English-French Dictionary	4.50
Stein: German Exercises	.40
Sumichrast: Les Trois Mousquetaires	.70
Les Misérables	.00
Van Daell: Mémoires du Duc de Saint-Simon	.64

International Modern Language Series.

Bôcher: Original Texts.	
Le Misantrope (Molière)	.20
De L'Institution des Enfans (Montaigne)	.20
Andromaque (Racine)	.20
Boïelle: Quatrevingt-Treize (Hugo)	.60
Freeborn: Morceaux Choisis de Daudet. (Authorized Edition)	.00
Kimball: La Famille de Germandre (Sand)	.50
Luquiens: French Prose: Popular Science	.60
French Prose: La Prise de la Bastille (Michelet)	.20
French Prose: Travels	.00
Paris: La Chanson de Roland (Extraits)	.60
Rollins: Madame Thérèse (Erckmann-Chatrian)	.60
Van Daell: La Cigale chez les Fourmis (Legouvé et Labiche)	.20
Introduction to the French Language	1.00
Bultmann: Soll und Haben (Freytag)	.60
Gore: Brigitta (Auerbach)	.00
Gruener: Dietegen (Keller)	.35
Nichols: Die Erhebung Europas gegen Napoleon I. (von Sybel)	.60
Wilson: Burg Neideck (Riehl)	.00

Copies sent to Teachers for Examination, with a view to Introduction, on receipt of Introduction Price.

GINN & COMPANY, Publishers,
BOSTON, NEW YORK, AND CHICAGO.

NATURAL SCIENCE TEXT-BOOKS.

ELEMENTS OF PHYSICS. A Text-book for High Schools and Academies. By ALFRED P. GAGE, A.M., Instructor in Physics in the English High School, Boston. $1.12.

C. F. **Emerson**, *Prof. of Physics, Dartmouth College:* "It takes up the subject on the right plan, and presents it in a clear yet scientific way."

INTRODUCTION TO PHYSICAL SCIENCE. By A. P. GAGE, author of "Elements of Physics." $1.00.

B. F. **Sharpe**, *Prof. of Natural Science, Randolph-Macon College, Va.:* "It is the very thing for the academy preparatory to this college."

PHYSICAL LABORATORY MANUAL AND NOTE-BOOK. By A. P. GAGE, author of "Elements of Physics," "Introduction to Physical Science," etc. 35 cents.

I. Thornton **Osmond**, *Prof. of Physics, Penn. State College:* "It is a product of the ability, experience, and sound judgment that have made Dr. Gage's other books the best of their rank in physics."

INTRODUCTION TO CHEMICAL SCIENCE. By R. P. WILLIAMS, Instructor in Chemistry in the English High School, Boston. 80 cents.

Arthur B. **Willmot**, *Prof. of Chemistry, Antioch College, Ohio:* "It is the best chemistry I know of for high-school work."

LABORATORY MANUAL OF GENERAL CHEMISTRY. By R. P. WILLIAMS, author of "Introduction to Chemical Science." 25 cents.

W. M. **Stine**, *Prof. of Chemistry, Ohio University, Athens, Ohio:* "It is a work that has my heartiest indorsement. I consider it thoroughly pedagogical in its principles."

YOUNG'S GENERAL ASTRONOMY. A Text-book for Colleges and Technical Schools. By CHARLES A. YOUNG, Ph.D., LL.D., Prof. of Astronomy in Princeton College, and author of "The Sun," etc. $2.25.

S. P. **Langley**, *Sec. Smithsonian Institution, Wash., D.C., and Pres. National Academy of Sciences:* "I know no better book (not to say as good a one) for its purpose on the subject."

YOUNG'S ELEMENTS OF ASTRONOMY. A Text-book for Use in High Schools and Academies, with a Uranography. By CHARLES A. YOUNG, author of "Young's General Astronomy," "The Sun," etc. $1.40. **Uranography.** From "Young's Elements of Astronomy." 30 cents.

S. H. **Brackett**, *Teacher of Mathematics, St. Johnsbury Academy, Vt.:* "It is just what I expected it would be, the very best which I have ever seen."

YOUNG'S LESSONS IN ASTRONOMY. Including Uranography. By CHARLES A. YOUNG, author of "A General Astronomy," of "Elements of Astronomy," etc. Prepared for schools that desire a brief course free from mathematics. $1.20.

AN INTRODUCTION TO SPHERICAL AND PRACTICAL ASTRONOMY. By DASCOM GREENE, Prof. of Mathematics and Astronomy in the Rensselaer Polytechnic Institute, Troy, N.Y. $1.50.

Davis **Garber**, *Prof. of Astronomy, Muhlenberg College:* "Students pursuing astronomy on a practical line will find it a very excellent and useful book."

ELEMENTS OF STRUCTURAL AND SYSTEMATIC BOTANY. For High Schools and Elementary College Courses. By DOUGLAS HOUGHTON CAMPBELL, Ph.D., Prof. of Botany in the Indiana University. $1.12.

Charles W. **Dodge**, *Teacher of Botany, High School, Detroit, Mich.:* "It is the only English work at all satisfactory for high-school students."

BLAISDELL'S PHYSIOLOGIES: Our Bodies and How We Live, 65 cents; **How to Keep Well**, 45 cents; **Child's Book of Health**, 30 cents.

True, scientific, interesting, teachable.

ELEMENTARY METEOROLOGY. By WILLIAM M. DAVIS, Prof. of Physical Geography in Harvard University. With maps, charts, and exercises. $2.50.

Copies will be sent, post paid, to teachers for examination on receipt of the introduction prices given above.

GINN & COMPANY, Publishers.
BOSTON. NEW YORK. CHICAGO. LONDON.

BOOKS IN HIGHER ENGLISH.

		Introd. Price.
Alexander:	Introduction to Browning	$1.00
Athenæum Press Series:		
	Cook: Sidney's Defense of Poesy	.80
	Gummere: Old English Ballads	.00
	Schelling: Ben Jonson's Timber	.80
Baker:	Plot-Book of Some Elizabethan Plays	.00
Cook:	A First Book in Old English	1.50
	Shelley's Defense of Poetry	.50
	The Art of Poetry	1.12
	Hunt's What is Poetry?	.50
	Newman's Aristotle's Poetics	.30
	Addison's Criticisms on Paradise Lost	1.00
	Bacon's Advancement of Learning	.00
Corson:	Primer of English Verse	1.00
Emery:	Notes on English Literature	1.00
English Literature Pamphlets:	Ancient Mariner, .05; First Bunker Hill Address, .10; Essay on Lord Clive, .15; Second Essay on the Earl of Chatham, .15; Burke, I. and II.; Webster, I. and II.; Bacon; Wordsworth, I. and II.; Coleridge and Burns; Addison and Goldsmith . . . . . Each	.15
Fulton & Trueblood:	Practical Elocution . . . . . Retail	1.50
	Choice Readings, $1.50; Chart of Vocal Expression	2.00
	College Critic's Tablet	.60
Garnett:	English Prose from Elizabeth to Victoria	1.50
Gayley:	Classic Myths in English Literature	1.50
Genung:	Outlines of Rhetoric	1.00
	Elements of Rhetoric, $1.25; Rhetorical Analysis	1.12
Gummere:	Handbook of Poetics	1.00
Hudson:	Harvard Edition of Shakespeare's Complete Works:—	
	20 Vol. Ed. Cloth, retail, $25.00; Half-calf, retail	55.00
	10 Vol. Ed. Cloth, retail, $20.00; Half-calf, retail	40.00
	Life, Art, and Characters of Shakespeare. 2 vols. Cloth	4.00
	New School Shakespeare. Each play: Paper, .30; Cloth	.45
	Text-Book of Poetry; Text-Book of Prose . . Each	1.25
	Classical English Reader	1.00
Lockwood:	Lessons in English, $1.12; Thanatopsis	.10
Maxcy:	Tragedy of Hamlet	.45
Minto:	Manual of English Prose Literature	1.50
	Characteristics of English Poets	1.50
Newcomer:	Practical Course in English Composition	.80
Phelps:	English Romantic Movement	1.00
Sherman:	Analytics of Literature	1.25
Smith:	Synopsis of English and American Literature	.80
Sprague:	Milton's Paradise Lost and Lycidas	.45
Thayer:	The Best Elizabethan Plays	1.25
Thom:	Shakespeare and Chaucer Examinations	1.00
White:	Philosophy of American Literature	.30
Whitney:	Essentials of English Grammar	.75
Whitney & Lockwood:	English Grammar	.70
Winchester:	Five Short Courses of Reading in English Literature	.40

AND OTHER VALUABLE WORKS.

GINN & COMPANY, Publishers,
Boston, New York, and Chicago.

www.ingramcontent.com/pod-product-compliance
Lightning Source LLC
Chambersburg PA
CBHW031449160426
43195CB00010BB/914